ONE YEAR AT THE
RUSSIAN COURT: 1904-1905

Copyright © 2018 Read Books Ltd.
This book is copyright and may not be
reproduced or copied in any way without
the express permission of the publisher in writing

British Library Cataloguing-in-Publication Data
A catalogue record for this book is available from
the British Library

THE EX-EMPRESS ALEXANDRA FEODOROVNA OF RUSSIA
WITH THE EX-TZAREVITCH ALEXIS

ONE YEAR AT THE RUSSIAN COURT: 1904-1905
BY RENÉE ELTON MAUD

CONTENTS

PART I
THE FULFILMENT OF MY DREAM . . .   PAGE 1

PART II
IN THE CAUCASUS 79

PART III
AT PETROGRAD 105

PART IV
RASPUTIN : HIS INFLUENCE AND HIS WORK . 189

LIST OF ILLUSTRATIONS

THE EX-EMPRESS ALEXANDRA FEODOROVNA OF RUSSIA WITH THE EX-CZAREVITCH ALEXIS . . . . . . *Frontispiece*

                                                    FACING PAGE

RUSSIAN COACHMAN 6

CAUCASUS—GOURIAN PRINCE 6

RUSSIAN EQUIPAGES—TWO TROÏKAS . . 7

IN THE PARK OF MONREPOS—THE FERRY TO LUDWINSTEIN 14

MONREPOS—THE CHAR-À-BANCS . . . 15

THE CASTLE OF MONREPOS FROM THE PARK . 22

PETERHOF—THE IMPERIAL CHILDREN . . 23

CRONSTADT—TWO SURVIVORS OF THE GLORIOUS KOREITZ 62

THE BARRACKS AT PETERHOF—TWO COSSACKS OF THE ESCORT 62

THE CROWN PRINCE OF GERMANY WITH PRINCESS CECILIE AS FIANCÉS 63

	FACING PAGE
SCENERY IN THE CAUCASUS	90
IN THE MOUNTAINS OF THE CAUCASUS	91
TIFLIS—A PERSIAN BAKER'S SHOP	94
TIFLIS—A PERSIAN SHOEMAKER'S SHOP	95
PLOUGHING IN THE CAUCASUS	216
THE IMPERIAL PALACE OF TZARSKOË-CELO	217

Part I
THE FULFILMENT OF MY DREAM

CHAPTER I

AT last, I was on the eve of my departure for Russia! The dream of my twenty summers! For that great Russia, the country of my devoted grandmother, Baroness de Nicolay, who, however, was born in London, her father, Baron de Nicolay, being at the time attached to the Russian Embassy there. He subsequently became Russian Minister at Copenhagen, where on account of the many friendships he had formed in society and his deep attachment to the then King and Queen of Denmark and all their family—who held him in the greatest esteem and intimacy— he remained more than twenty years, refusing every offer of advancement in consequence.

Queen Louise, Queen Alexandra's mother, kept up a frequent correspondence with my grandmother up to the time of the latter's death. Here, it may be of interest to mention that I have amongst my most valued possessions a beautiful diamond bracelet given by the Queen to my grandmother, who was by birth half French on her mother's side, *née* Princesse de Broglie-Revel, and until her marriage maid of honour to the Empress of Russia. That great Russia, the charms and delights of which in my innermost self I had longed for and at night dreamt of, during the long winter months passed in the solitude of my ancient and austere Norman home, listening to the howling of the wind amongst the pine trees as they groaned and bent their heads in cadence. How good it was to dream then!

Years after my Uncle Auguste de Villaine, my father's brother, was specially requested by the King and Queen of Denmark, in remembrance of the past, to be sent as French Military Attaché to Copenhagen.

The husband of my friend Madame de Saint-Pair had just been appointed Naval Attaché at St Petersburg (Petrograd), and I obtained my father's permission to accompany her on her journey to rejoin her husband. First of all I was to pay a visit to my aunt, Baroness de Nicolay, who was waiting to receive me.

On reaching the Russian Frontier, at Wirballen, at 8.30 p.m., we had to change from the North Express into the Russian train on account of the gauge being much wider in the land of the Tzar—as it was then. No sooner had the train come to a standstill than our compartment was literally invaded by a crowd of porters —at least one for each of our packages! The train which had been so full on leaving Paris was by this time almost empty—hence the reason for this invasion, each one fighting as to which should bear the burden! Dressed in those curiously long coats caught up in pleats at the waist, with their baggy trousers, top boots, flat caps and white aprons reaching to

THE FULFILMENT OF MY DREAM 5

the knee, as they walked about on the station platform with their hands behind their backs, they looked like male hospital nurses.

Thanks to the very special recommendation of the Russian Ambassador in Paris and, in spite of the fierce expression worn by the tall, pompous and bewhiskered Colonel of the Gendarmes, this very important functionary merely bowed to our luggage allowing it all to pass the customs without being examined. Many jealous eyes must have watched us there, for the Russian Customs were most severe.

I noticed a large picture of the Sacred Heart with a huge candle burning in front of it—I was indeed in Holy Russia.

An amusing incident occurred on the arrival of the train at Gatchina, where Her Imperial Majesty the Dowager-Empress had a palace, which I feel I must relate. From the windows of our compartment we were able to get a peep at the Grand Duke Nicholas-Michaelovitch, who had just left our train for a dressing-room in the station, and witnessed in silence the transformation of a Grand Duke from civilian clothes into the uniform of his rank, which is by no means a small affair—but I must say a quick one!

A few minutes later we saw His Imperial Highness dashing away in a brilliant Court equipage, his attendants in Imperial scarlet liveries. This was certainly my first experience of a Grand Duke in such complete *négligé*.

At Petrograd my aunt's brougham was awaiting me. A Russian turn-out is delightfully picturesque. The coachman is dressed in a long dark blue padded coat, especially thick in winter; his vast proportions completely fill up the whole box-seat and sometimes even overlap it. The fatter he looks, the smarter he is. He wears a very full skirt and, with his face framed by his long hair, his top hat cut short, his waist-belt of many colours, his fashion of driving with both his arms stretched out at full length in front of him, and instead of using a whip—which is non-existent—occasionally calling out in guttural tones, he forms a truly picturesque object to the visitors from foreign lands.

There is yet another type of coachman, seen more seldom, however, who is dressed as a Russian postilion and who in summer wears long silk sleeves of varied brilliant hues issuing from his dark coat. The top of his round toque is edged with short up-standing peacock feathers. The big, black, sure-footed, nervous horses, with their long tails and manes, do not resemble ours in any way. The reins and the red or blue tassels brighten up the harness, and how enjoyable it is to go for a drive in a sleigh at full tilt, zigzagging about over the pure white snow as slippery as glass, specially so in a troïka, to the tinkling sound of its many bells. But, in a droschki, with its narrow borderless seat, the only alternative is to seize one's companion's waist; it may have its charm also!

My Aunt de Nicolay—Tante Sonine, as I always called her—*née* Baroness de Meyendorff, had frequented all the most brilliant Courts of

RUSSIAN COACHMAN

CAUCASUS—GOURIAN PRINCE

RUSSIAN EQUIPAGES—TWO TROÏKAS (THREE HORSES)

Europe, being well known both in London and Berlin. Being married at the age of eighteen to my uncle, my grandmother's brother, she had accompanied her husband during his entire diplomatic career—necessarily a somewhat nomadic existence. My aunt welcomed me with much warmth, which touched me profoundly. I had met her for the first time in 1900 on the occasion of her visit to Paris at the time of the Great Exhibition, after which she had come to Normandy, and it was during this visit that I began to form for her that deep admiration and affection which her memory will always invoke in me.

My aunt was altogether charming; tall and very distinguished looking, and extraordinarily refined—in fact a real *grande dame* to her fingertips. She appeared to be much younger than she was. Her beautiful features had preserved a wonderfully youthful charm, to be seen at their full value when she smiled that sweet smile of hers—so good and so true. I very soon began positively to adore her.

During her youth my aunt had been very pretty, with her dazzling fair hair and fresh pink and white complexion, so much so that at a great Court ball at the Winter Palace one of the Grand Dukes remarked: " She is not a woman, she is a swan ! "

Even at the time of my visit she still gave one this impression: she was so graceful in all her movements and as active and supple as any young woman of twenty-five ; and, to see her beautiful little head so proudly borne on her long flexible neck with its aristocratic lines attached to those exquisitely moulded shoulders of hers, one could imagine that she had simply sailed through life partaking of all its beauties and avoiding all contact with the horrors and pettiness of the great world she frequented, thus conserving intact, both in a moral and a physical sense, the pure whiteness of the " swan "!

Left a widow at thirty-two, my aunt was always an ideal mother, giving every proof of entire devotion to her children—her every thought was for them and theirs. Her voice, combining softness with firmness, was one of her most charming characteristics, with such a perfect pronunciation in French, English and German that a stranger would have asked himself which of the three was her native tongue.

She declared she did not know Russian well enough, and preferred never to speak in that language in society.

One of the first instructions I received from her was—" Always shake hands with a gentleman when he is presented." How different from the English custom, where a slight nod and side look often suffices! While in France a young girl is more demure still! Where a married woman is concerned in Russia, a man generally kisses her hand—which suits the Russian as much as it renders ridiculous the Frenchman when he tries to imitate.

Then, another day, she said to me looking rather upset at having to touch such a delicate subject: "Tu sais—on a beaucoup de cousins ici." This was said as a warning for me not to be shocked, as I might perhaps have been, at the sight of a somewhat too great familiarity between certain people on frequent occasion. This warning amused me intensely, as, although I was very innocent at the time, I was not sufficiently so not to understand the hint! I was simply charmed by the thought—more so still at the explanation and was never quite able to repress a smile when I came across " happy cousins "!

She always retained the best impressions of London life, having spent several years here. " Jews are very well received there," she once said to me, " very different from here." In fact, I think London is their Paradise, I am quite sure they are in no hurry for the accomplishment of the Gospel !

She informed me, much to my surprise, that the German woman was the most light of morals of any nation. Their heavy, massive appearance had always made me imagine them unable to see life but through heavily-rimmed spectacles and that the great majority of them followed the example of their homely plump Kaiserin and her three " K " doctrine for women—" Kinder, Kirche and Kuchen."

On my return to France my aunt accompanied me as far as Berlin and proved herself an excellent cicerone, pointing out to me the various palaces she had so often been received in and other places of interest. The only thing I could truthfully admire in the city was its scrupulous cleanliness. I beheld with horror these long rows of white "stucco" rulers of Germany erected by their descendent and admirer Wilhelm the Hun; neither was I impressed by that fearful crude blue light of the chapel containing the Imperial tombs—again a result of the imagination of the "All Highest." Clearly this decoration simply aimed at showy effect—just like every action he commits.

Although Petrograd is more primitive than Paris, yet it impressed me far more, with its wide arteries, its large quays, its superb Neva, like an arm of the sea.

Russia is the country of space, of dreams—the country of all that is magnificent. It gives one an unforgettable impression.

The Newsky Prospect is said to be the widest street in Europe; on one side of it is an ancient caravanserai of enormous dimensions, now occupied by shops of every description, some of which are most fascinating.

I was also taken to see the famous fortress of St Peter and St Paul, the burial place of the Russian sovereigns and also a prison, returning by steamer on the Neva, and then to the Hermitage—the National Gallery of Petrograd—containing many of Murillo's best works as well as Rembrandt's and others. Another day I went to the Alexander III. Museum and to the Church of Kazan where there is a most venerated statue of the Virgin. The Cathedral of St Isaac is of magnificent proportions and possesses immense

THE FULFILMENT OF MY DREAM

wealth of decoration—the mosaiques being superb, whilst a number of the sacred images are inlaid with diamonds and other precious stones.

During the course of my explorations, nothing struck me so forcibly in contrast to all this magnificence as the house of Peter the Great—which is so minute!

I thoroughly enjoyed going to the restaurants at The Islands, specially to Ernest's, where one meets natives, diplomats, foreign visitors, in fact, every one, while listening to the strains of a gay Rumanian orchestra.

The Islands are the Bois de Boulogne of Petrograd. The place is lovely: very green; beautiful trees overshadowing paths which are well laid out; and from the end of the park a view of the sea is obtainable. There are many beautiful villas there occupied during the summer.

I never shall forget my impressions of Paris on my return from Russia, where there seems to be no limit to space, where everything is on a huge scale—from the luxury of life in general to the immense size of all the buildings and the great width of the noble Neva. Paris appeared to me a squalid town and the Seine a mere brook—and not too clean a one either—and altogether it struck me as being a very dismal place.

I only spent then a very short time at Petrograd as, at that period of the year, every one begins to flit away to their country places for the summer, so, after having become acquainted with a number of relations and made several friends, I, like the rest, took my departure from the capital, and accompanied my aunt to her beautiful home of Monrepos in Finland.

CHAPTER II

THE country from Petrograd to Viborg is for the most part like one perpetual garden, the train passes between what is literally a long series of villas and gardens in the midst of silver birch and pine-trees, broken occasionally by an evident attempt to create a new place; then succeeds again a planted solitude; and at last, after a journey of four hours, Viborg—a town of 30,000 inhabitants—is reached.

That planted solitude has since those days become very much built over, I expect, as Finland is a very sought-after summer resort.

Finland—the country of the thousand lakes, or rather one ought to say of the five thousand lakes! My grandmother's land won my heart at once. Monrepos was for me a touching souvenir of her.

It is a well-known show place, with its lovely and hilly woodlands reaching down to the Gulf of Finland, its gorgeous flower-beds and standard orange-trees, where the coast is indented with its pink coloured rocks and in the background are interminable forests of pine and silver beech, where wolves come in winter. In one of the kiosks in the park is a marble bust of the Empress Maria, given by her to my great-grandfather to whom she was much attached. In the park there stands also a column erected to the memory of two Princes de Broglie who fell, fighting for the Allies, against Napoleon—these two princes were brothers of my great-grandmother. Another column was presented to my great-grandfather by the town of Viborg in recognition of a gift of land and other bequests made by him. Every corner contains some souvenir; every bench is named after a member of the family.

My aunt took me to visit the tomb of the Nicolays situated on one of the prettiest islands in the park, named the Isle of Ludwinstein, all formed of pink coloured rocks covered with lovely trees. To reach this poetic spot where the dear dead rest so peacefully, one effects the crossing of a narrow arm of the Gulf on a ferry bridge worked by ropes fastened at either end, by means of which one is enabled to pull oneself over the deeply-shaded waters of the beautiful Gulf of Finland. Ludwinstein dominates its full immensity interspersed by thickly-wooded islands; there the great northern sun bathes itself before setting in its multi-coloured glory. Then is the time to steal quietly away to think—and pray—on the island of Death and Life and Hope.

Finland is far more Swedish than Russian, having belonged to the Swedish Crown for so long, and Viborg was very animated; we often went there. The long drives into the country generally in the char-à-bancs were a great joy to me. My aunt's coachman, Kousma, besides

IN THE PARK OF MONREPOS, THE FERRY TO LUDWINSTEIN

MONREPOS—"THE CHAR-À-BANCS"

THE FULFILMENT OF MY DREAM

being a Tartar was also a Mussulman, and being a strict observer of the Koran had a bath in his room in which he performed his numerous obligatory ablutions. As Mussulmans are not allowed to drink any strong liquor, this being contrary to their faith, they are in great request as servants in Russia.

Another of my great amusements was to go for a sail in one or the other of my aunt's boats on the Gulf; and at times we used to row ourselves—a form of exercise which has always appealed to me.

The Catholic Church at Viborg was very small; the congregation consisted of about three to four hundred soldiers and a few peasant women, picturesque with their bright coloured—generally red—handkerchiefs on their heads. Whenever I entered the church these soldiers lined up on either side of the aisle in my honour. I almost imagined I was the Empress! But I never shall forget the smell of their top boots caused by the fat used for cleaning them. It was almost unbearable.

There is always a night watchman round the house, who chimes the hours all through the night and keeps a vigilant watch. Monrepos is entirely built of wood, after the fashion of so many large houses in Russia, but so strong and massive in construction that it is difficult to realize the absence of stone.

The house—the houses, I ought to say, for there are two—is of enormous dimensions and to give an illustration of this I may mention that the large drawing-room is more than 150 feet in length and very lofty.

My aunt always lived with her three unmarried children, Paul and his two sisters, Marie and Aline; it has always been my habit to call them " uncle " and " aunt " on account of their being so much older than myself and I thought it more respectful to do so. The first two are entirely devoted to good works and before the war my uncle was absolutely absorbed by the Œuvre des Étudiants, an international business, and as this body held their annual meetings in different places each year he was continually travelling, and thought no more of starting off to America or Japan than he did of going to Petrograd.

My young Pahlen cousins, children of the married daughter of my aunt, came to stay. I nicknamed them " Les Moustiques " as, all day long, they clambered on to my knees and then smothered me with kisses! Their father, Count de Pahlen, was then Governor of Vilna —now, alas, fallen into the hands of the detestable Hun! They played the balalaika—a cross between the mandoline and the guitar—very well.

Uncle de Pahlen, although a somewhat pronounced Protestant, was large-minded enough to rescue the Roman Catholic Bishop of Vilna, by concealing him in the bottom of his equipage, from the hands of the revolutionaries the following winter. All the Nicolays are very low church, with the exception of Uncle Paul who

THE FULFILMENT OF MY DREAM

admires and venerates God far more in nature than beneath the roof of any temple—so I was told.

The Finns' one idea was and still is to obtain an autonomy of their own—the Russian Governor of the Province was usually hated and I am right in stating that during my visit several attempts on his life were made.

When women received the right to vote in Finland, the accomplishment of this achievement was the cause of a frenzy of delight.

We were always a large party at Monrepos, a perpetual coming and going of friends. On the occasion of the visit of my French friends, Monsieur and Madame de Saint-Pair, we had arranged together to visit Imatra, the famous waterfalls of which are known the world over. The great fall is superb—the foam reaching to an immense height—but I prefer the smaller fall, although it is stiller but a good deal wider than the great fall.

It happened to be the feast of St John, in celebration of which huge bonfires are lit all over the country. We did not actually see the midnight sun, as we were not quite far enough north for that, but it was 11.30 p.m. before the afterglow entirely vanished. Then we went to see a country dance undertaken amidst profound silence, the Finn takes his pleasures quietly! I noticed that all the men of the dance wore small daggers in their belts, no doubt to protect their belles, I concluded; and the latter certainly were remarkable for the wonderful dazzling brightness of their fair hair plaited in thick tresses of wonderful richness.

On our return to the inn we were served with a whole ham cut in the form of a duck, and radishes to represent flowers, while the butter took the shape of sea anemones.

The following morning we drove 36 kilometres in a carriage which looked more like a hearse than anything else, with no springs, and drawn by three horses who took the bits between their mouths and galloped for all they were worth along a road like a switchback, only worse, on account of the innumerable deep ruts all over it, and in some places edged with real precipices. Naturally the vehicle possessed no brake!

The country is very wild, full of woods and thick undergrowth on either side of the road; then, wooded hills and a few cottages here and there; pines and birch-trees everywhere.

Our hearse-shaped conveyance certainly possessed the semblance of a roof, but the planks of wood composing it did not fit, with the result that we were obliged to open our umbrellas inside to prevent ourselves from being soaked by the heavy rain occasioned by a severe thunderstorm which overtook us, on this never-to-be-forgotten excursion in the wildest and most romantic parts of the country. The little boys on the road blew us kisses, while the little girls offered us fruit, flowers, eggs, and pretty coloured stones.

On arrival at Rättijärvi we took the steamer down the canal of Lake Saima, thoroughly enjoying the lovely scenery by which we were surrounded, as we passed on our way through many lakes.

The locks of Juustila are very interesting—our boat sunk deeper and deeper, so deep indeed that I thought we would never reach the bottom ! We returned enchanted with our Finnish trip.

At Monrepos, we had some charming neighbours, amongst whom were the Count and Countess de Stackelberg. The latter was before her marriage Countess Shouvaloff, a niece of my aunt and the daughter of a former Russian Ambassador at Berlin, while her husband, General Baron de Stackelberg, was attached to the person of one of the Grand Dukes. I have often met them in Paris since those days, and to my great regret I heard lately that at the outbreak of the late revolution in March 1917 Count Stackelberg was arrested and was actually being led off to the Bureau Central by a detachment of soldiers to be tried, when, while still on his own staircase, a shot was fired—presumably by some ill-advised person, at the top of the staircase—whereupon the soldiers, who were on the ground-floor and far from the unfortunate General who was unarmed, imagining that it was he who had fired at them, turned on him with violence and finally shot him in cold blood.

Half an hour after this tragedy my uncle, Baron Paul de Nicolay, called at the house, when he also was arrested by a young revolutionary who left him in charge of two soldiers while he went off to fetch his revolver. The soldiers' attention being taken away by their leader's action, my uncle profited by their momentary distraction and most fortunately was thus enabled to make good his escape, otherwise he would most probably have shared the same fate as poor Stackelberg.

I have the greatest affection for Uncle Paul, from whom I often receive long and most interesting letters, which help to remind me of the happy days I am now attempting to describe—the golden memory of which will ever remain impressed upon my heart.

It is to be hoped that Fate will spare Finland and the cradle of the family from an invasion by the brutal Hun, and may the Angel of Peace protect those blessed tombs from his sacrilegious and infamous hands.

I left Finland to go back to Petrograd with my aunt for a few days, which I spent most gaily. Then I went to Peterhof with my aunt, Princess Cherwachidze, and to Michaelovka with Aunt de Baranoff, going often from one to the other.

CHAPTER III

THE Court spent the summer at the Palace of Peterhof. My aunt, Princess Cherwachidze, always rented a villa there on leaving her house at Petrograd. Most of the Grand Dukes had their palaces there also. Being only at a distance of about one hour by train from Petrograd, Peterhof with its numerous palaces and villas, situated in their lovely gardens, reminded me of the Riviera; by its brilliant society, both military and civil, Peterhof was indeed a delightful place to live in. There was a perpetual round of luncheons and dinners in the Court Circle which I enjoyed very much, also the concerts and the theatre.

The place is charmingly pretty; the park magnificent, reaching right down to the shores of the Baltic where many of its fine trees dip their long branches into the sea. In the park we used to meet the Imperial Children, Grand Duchess Olga, the eldest, and lately one of the leading sister-disciples of Rasputin's religion, was then a pretty little doll, always very gracious and well-dressed. She used to say "Bonjour" aloud when anyone bowed to her; policemen and others were delighted with the salutation of their "little Empress!" Later on, their drives and rides had to be discontinued as attempts on their lives were feared.

The second daughter, Grand Duchess Tatiana, was said to be the cleverest of the family and her father's favourite.

The playing of the fountains was a sight worth seeing, the Russians never ceased asking me whether they did not outshine the " Grandes Eaux " of Versailles.

The appearance of the exterior of the Palace inspired gaiety, whilst the interior was the very acme of comfort.

The Russian Court was the most luxurious Court in the world, combining as it did all the wealth and luxury of the East and the West. It was a rule that all the numerous palaces of the Emperor should be kept up during his absence just as though he were in residence— always ready to receive him at any moment.

I often accompanied my aunt to the Palace of Peterhof to see my uncle, Prince Cherwachidze, who was Grand Master of the Court of Russia, specially attached to the person of the Empress-Dowager, being also Grand Master of her Court ; and he sometimes came to spend his evenings with us.

My aunt continually lunched with the Empress-Dowager, who used to invite her every year to spend long friendly visits with her at Gatchina ; she also lunched very often at the Palace. My aunt might have taken up her abode in the Palace had she chosen, but always declared she preferred her liberty to the perpetual glow and

THE CASTLE OF MONREPOS FROM THE PARK

PETERHOF, THE IMPERIAL CHILDREN

THE FULFILMENT OF MY DREAM 23

fuss of the Court—in my view a somewhat injudicious step to have taken considering all things.

Princess Cherwachidze, *née* Baronne de Nicolay, my father's first cousin, is small and slender, very refined and fragile, so fragile indeed that one is almost afraid of breaking her when embracing her, but possessing in her heart an unfathomable depth of kindness and devotion.

My dear little aunt—Aunt Maka, as I called her—seemed to be in love, so much in love with her husband that morning and night, especially when at Petrograd, she rushed off as fast as she could cover the ground to the telephone to converse with the object of her adoration, who was always in waiting on his Imperial Mistress wherever she happened to be — Gatchina, Peterhof, Tsarskoe-Celo or Petrograd, at the Anitschkoff Palace. The conversation was always the same and in her soft emotional voice she commenced :—

" Comment vas-tu ? " The reply I never caught. " Allons tant mieux." Idem. " Tu vas venir aujourd'hui, n'est-ce pas ? " I guessed the reply to be in the negative. " Et demain ? " Again in the negative. " Alors tu me diras. Au revoir." Then it was over. He was not often able to respond to these summonses.

She seemed quite satisfied to know that her spouse was in good health—there was no alternative—and then again would rush off across the drawing-rooms back to her comfortable study where she always had a vast correspondence to attend to, and to reply to in that beautiful caligraphy of hers—everything she undertook to do was executed to perfection. Every day she received several begging letters, some from people desirous of obtaining employment, others seeking for Imperial audiences for some protégé or other—and these latter simply poured in !

Again at night, she used to ring up my uncle on the telephone which, alas, more often than not gave no reply ; then my poor little aunt became quite thoughtful and sadly consoled herself by saying, " Comme son service est fatiguant ! "

She had also a conversation on the telephone very often with Grand Duke Nicholas Michaelovitch who had been a friend of hers for many years. His Imperial Highness sometimes came to see us in the evening and we always knew when he had entered the apartment by the tremendous clatter of his scabbard on the parquet floor of the ante-room and the clinking of his spurs as he walked. He was of a jovial disposition and spoke with a very loud voice. He was besides *un gai causeur* and extremely literary, amongst his last publications was *La Famille des Strogonoff*.

Every morning, dressed as simply as possible, and wearing a little black felt hat with a tiny little ruffled up feather and carrying a small black leather bag, my aunt used to go out on missions of charity ; the felt was no longer very new, neither was the feather, but that mattered not at all to my dear little aunt.

Ordinary—and extraordinary—confessor to all

THE FULFILMENT OF MY DREAM 25

the troubled consciences which chose to make her house their meeting place, nothing struck me as being more strangely dissimilar than this immaculate soul—almost unique beneath the snow-laden sky of this frozen country—to those who invaded the blessed atmosphere of that drawing-room, pouring out all their griefs and faults into her ever-sympathetic ears.

The Prince was less sentimental. Spoilt by a great fortune, occupying a high post at Court, his presence at home became less and less until there seemed no real reason to bind him to it at all, and yet, when he did happen to come, he seemed so happy. But it was extremely difficult for anyone to read exactly the innermost thoughts of my dear uncle, who belongs to a very good old princely family of Georgia; he is a Caucasian, and consequently portrays in his character all the mystery of his race, to a greater degree even than the Slav. He has a somewhat striking appearance with his large dark eyes. He is very gracious, when he chooses, and unequalled in the art of finesse, morally speaking.

Although his thoughts were nearly always in the clouds, they occasionally issued from their nebulous seclusion, but never for long. This originality seemed to please his Sovereign Lady and some people used to conceive this to be the cause of the high favour in which he stood.

At official ceremonies my uncle, in his magnificent gold uniform all covered with Ribbons and Orders, appeared to emerge from the midst of those yards of shimmering velvet or silk which formed the train of the Empress-Dowager and which seemed to take pleasure in rustling all the more at his touch. He cut a superb figure as he sat in his Court carriage, wearing his fine cocked hat surmounted with white plumes, and on the box seat the men in Royal scarlet and gold liveries with their gold-gallooned hats slightly tilted to one side—the whole being drawn by a pair of high-stepping greys.

At Peterhof we often used to drive in this fine turn-out, and many were the low obeisances bestowed on us by respectful functionaries as we passed.

Tongues were very busy on the subject of my uncle and I could not but feel a little sad for my aunt. It was with eyes closed and with her heart brim-full of him that she used to visit a certain perfidious beauty enjoying the liberty of grass widowhood—her husband being at the war—and I felt sure that the lady knew more about my uncle during her brief acquaintance with him than did my dear good credulous aunt during the whole of her twenty-five years of legitimate married life. But perhaps my youthful imagination ran riot and judging from what people whispered you may think jealousy is as rampant in Russia as it is here.

Queen Alexandra arrived at Peterhof during my sojourn there to spend a few days with her sister, the Empress-Dowager, and I remember so well seeing her. A cordon of sentinels had been drawn only a few paces apart all round the

THE FULFILMENT OF MY DREAM 27

Park interspersed with mounted Cossacks. My uncle has a profound admiration for the Rose Queen, who has held him in great esteem for many years. In the old days, when the world was normal, he used to meet Her Majesty at Copenhagen every year, where she always presented him with the latest photograph of herself, signed by her Royal hand—and at Petrograd he had a regular gallery of these.

My uncle is entirely devoted to the Empress and she will never let him out of her sight for long, giving him her full confidence; but, as he is a very bad sailor and dreads the long sea voyages, he always obtained her Imperial sanction to travel by way of Germany; so as to avoid sea-sickness as much as possible and for this purpose he wears a pair of red glasses. May this be a hint in future to all those who suffer from *mal de mer*!

He is still attached to the person of his Imperial Mistress, in the Crimea, and now sharing her life in misfortune with as much devotion as in former days. I feel sure he will never willingly consent to abandon her as in all probability she has been forsaken by so many.

On one occasion, while at Copenhagen, a little scandal was spread about in which the name of a certain very pretty maid of honour, who for the fun of the thing mischievous people wished to compromise, and that of my uncle, amongst others, were coupled. The papers, of course, got hold of the story and naturally exaggerated the whole event.

The Empress was furious and outraged at the mere suggestion of such a thing and in a loud voice protested, saying, " Le Prince n'y était pas, le Prince était chez moi." Now, the hour mentioned was one in which Morpheus makes one forget the sad hours when he no longer holds sway—and it was good of the Empress to champion her hero thus. People smiled but held their peace !

As every one knows, the greatest love and affection exist between our lovely Queen Alexandra and her sister. Since these Russian days I have often been to see my uncle in London, both at Buckingham Palace and, since King Edward's death, at Marlborough House, during the Empress's visits to the Queen, which during King Edward's lifetime usually took place when he was abroad on his several diplomatic missions, causing him to be recognized as Edward the Peacemaker. How richly he deserved that appellation is to be shown in the great result he achieved in bringing about the Entente Cordiale —as though he foresaw the present cataclysm— thus laying the foundation of the great brotherhood in arms which now exists between France and her old antagonist England in their common determination to crush the loathsome beast— the abominable Hun—in a life or death struggle. May time only strengthen this great alliance, is the heartfelt desire of one amongst thousands of the daughters of France.

At Buckingham Palace my uncle occupied a charming apartment just above the Visitors'

THE FULFILMENT OF MY DREAM 29

Entrance, though at Marlborough House his installation was naturally less sumptuous. There I was greeted at the top of the stairs by two giant Cossacks, the Cossacks of the Empress.

As my uncle experiences a good deal of difficulty in speaking English, the long sojourn in our midst used to get rather on his nerves, especially after King Edward died, as it was so hard for Queen Alexandra to reconcile herself to parting with her Imperial sister. Whenever the Empress thought of departure, the Queen threw herself into the Empress's arms and begged her to remain—and remain she did. Neither did the visits to Sandringham satisfy my uncle, who was only really happy in one place and that place was Copenhagen—where he seemed to become young again! quite young! I was told. My uncle took his place in the funeral procession of the late King Edward as one of the Russian delegates on that solemn occasion.

On his last visit to London, soon after my marriage, my husband and I saw a great deal of my uncle, with whom we often used to lunch at Buckingham Palace Hotel where he had a lovely suite of apartments on the first floor, because, as he used to say, " I am freer here than at Marlborough House." And he seemed to revel in the idea of his own *garçonnière*, although he had his room at Marlborough House as well.

That year the Empress remained in England until the last day of July, and was travelling on her way back to Russia through Germany on the day Russia actually declared war. On her arrival at Berlin the Imperial bomb-proof train was not allowed to continue any further east, but was ordered either to go back whence it came, namely to Calais, or else proceed to Denmark, as German Authorities felt sure she was conveying important messages from the King to his cousin the Tzar.

Her Imperial Majesty chose the latter route, thinking it would be the best way home later on.

My uncle also showed us a very pretty miniature of the Empress-Dowager given to him lately by Queen Alexandra, a charming thought for which he seemed very grateful.

He had sent to Petrograd for an enormous box of delicious bonbons which he gave us, they are so luscious there, and to ensure getting a good cup of tea when he came to see us, I expect, he presented us with some excellent green Russian tea.

CHAPTER IV

THE first great important ceremony which I attended was the funeral of General Obroutcheff, a great dignitary of the Empire.

The ceremony took place at La Laure, which is the ecclesiastical quarter of Petrograd and is an enormous monastery surrounded by walls and ditches full of water, a kind of fortified place—in fact, a town.

It contains a large cemetery, beautiful gardens and no less than seven churches. The monks, of whom there are a great number, wear long and very wide black cassocks with a sort of high hat widening toward the top. All of them let their hair and often their beards grow long; with some the hair reaches to the waist and is an object of great care. At night, the monks stand one behind the other plaiting each other's hair, which is generally curled and waved.

The popes are the secular and parish priests, and are married. Popes are in a certain degree a race of people apart; their children intermarry, the sons often become popes themselves. They are not generally much esteemed and the common saying is: " Pope, son of a dog!" As I have said, a pope can enter the married state, but only once in a life-time.

The police cordon was drawn as tight as possible. Quite close to us was the officer of the police with a sullen look and a livid complexion who took note of every one.

Presently the remainder of the guests arrived and the funeral procession itself appeared, the uniforms were superb and the *coup d'œil* a magnificent one.

All the Grand Dukes were there, amongst whom I recognized Alexis, George, Oldenburg, and the Court dignitaries, including my uncle Prince Cherwachidze, in full uniform, all covered with gold, the various Ambassadors, wearing only Russian decorations on this occasion, but such a profusion of them!

The Emperor and his brother—then the heir to the throne, for the Tzarevitch was not born—with the Empress-Dowager entered the church, after the celebration of Mass, for the committal service and took up their positions quite close to me, to the right of the Sanctuary, so close indeed that stretching out my hand I could have touched them

On the arrival of the Emperor and Empress at the Church the whole congregation bowed as the Imperial pair passed to their seats. There they were duly incensed, the Tzar's brother only receiving one incensing and accordingly only gave one inclination.

The Emperor appeared very shy and nervous with a somewhat frightened expression. The Empress-Dowager is short and dark, she has nothing of the beauty of her sister, Queen

THE FULFILMENT OF MY DREAM 33

Alexandra. The Tzar's brother is tall and fair with very blue eyes. He is a great sportsman and so strong that he can lift Prince Cherwachidze up as easily as a feather. He was very popular I believe.

The singing was wonderful, although unaccompanied by musical instruments as is customary in the Russian Church. I was carried away by it. The priests' vestments were incomparably rich, all white and gold—no trace of black anywhere. It is the custom of the Greek Church for even funeral hearses to be gilded or silvered, but never black as with us. It is also a rule that the corpse should be exposed in an open coffin during the religious ceremony, but in the case of the defunct general, who had died at his wife's home in France—she being French—this form was dispensed with.

That night, on our return to Peterhof I accompanied my Aunt Cherwachidze to a dinner given at Michaelovka by Grand Duke Michael-Michaelovitch, uncle of the Tzar. At this dinner were present Grand Duchess of Mecklenburg-Schwerin, with her daughter Princess Cecilie, now Crown Princess of Prussia, the Grand Duchess Xenia, sister of the Emperor, and others.

The previous evening I had dined with my friends the Saint-Pairs at the famous Ernest Restaurant on the Islands, the other guests including Prince and Princess Kotchoubey, the Prince has a very Turkish appearance and looks extremely flighty, while the Princess possesses a most wonderful figure, but is very made up

c

with her hair dyed gold; she has fine eyes but they lack lustre; the Swedish Minister and Countess Gyldenstolpe, who since then they have been to Paris many years in the same capacity, where I have seen a good deal of them, Countess Gyldenstolpe being a Miss Plunkett, a daughter of a former English Ambassador, both very distinguished looking and charming. Monsieur Lefèvre-Pontalis, Vicomte et Vicomtesse de Guichen and Vicomte de Salignac-Fénelon, all of the French Embassy, made up the party, which took place in a huge recess on the first floor overlooking the restaurant and just opposite the Rumanian orchestra which was playing gaily.

The table was beautifully decorated with pink roses and ilex and lighted by a profusion of prettily-shaded candles and electric lamps.

This was my first large dinner-party in Petrograd, which was to be followed so often by others. I enjoyed it thoroughly.

I returned to Petrograd a few days later with Princess Lise Bagration-Moncransky—a great friend of my Aunt Cherwachidze—then staying with us. After an excellent lunch at the Hôtel de l'Europe, then the smartest in Petrograd, he went off to see a Red Cross train on the point of leaving for Manchuria, everybody being interested at that time in the poignant question of the Russo-Japanese war—especially so, as we only received news from the war zone by way of Japan I was told. Princess Obolensky did the honours of her hospital train

THE FULFILMENT OF MY DREAM

showing us all the details, which were very complete.

The train was entirely painted in white with huge red crosses at intervals. What a good target it would have been for the modern German marksman!.

It was immensely long, being able to accommodate 300 people, including doctors, sisters of charity, and hospital attendants, and there was room for twenty-five officers. The medical corps were most comfortably installed, their study being so cosy—the writing-tables covered with green baize—so suitably furnished; charming little holy images with lamps burning in front of them were in every compartment.

The sisters of charity slept two in each room, their beds folded up as in ordinary " sleepers "—simplicity was the order of the day in this department. But the men were thoroughly spoilt, having a club room all to themselves, a fact which often makes me exclaim : " On voit bien que le Créateur était un homme."

There were four carriages set aside for slightly wounded cases, and I thought to myself the poor soldiers would suffer from being overcrowded—the beds being so close together. On each bed were a pair of leather slippers, a pair of socks and a grey woollen shirt. Crutches were placed at intervals for the use of convalescents.

Then followed the quarters for the serious cases with very fine mosquito nets in front of each window. The train was bomb proof, but I noticed the absence of iron shutters or any shutters at all, which struck me as being a great omission. These cases would enjoy more space and their beds could be easily removed as they were only stretchers.

There were two stories to this part of the train—quite like a house on wheels—icons and pious books were in great profusion. There were also a pharmacy and an operating room well stocked with every modern appliance.

The officers' beds were entirely covered with white mosquito nets and there were also head nets. We were shown the place where the linen was washed and disinfected. No money seemed to have been spared in the installation of this luxurious train, and I cannot help wondering what has been its destiny and how many poor suffering creatures it helped towards the alleviation of their pains.

The Hun takes as much pleasure in destroying the Red Cross as he does in finishing off the wounded on the battlefield; and I can only hope those who fought and died in 1904 did not encounter the same barbarous treatment at the hands of their enemies as those brave men who are in deadly contest now with the disciples of Kultur.

I was seized with a great desire to accompany Madame Narischkine, a friend of my Aunt de Nicolay, to Irkoutz, where she intended to go in order to nurse convalescents after her cure at the Eaux-Bonnes in France—Russians are always taking cures and they go across Europe as easily as we do from London to Brighton.

She was already a middle-aged woman, but very refined-looking. There was only one thing about her which rather spoilt her appearance, and that was that her fingers were very much stained with tobacco, and her teeth, too, from smoking cigarettes. In this she merely followed the example of the majority of Russian ladies, amongst whom smoking often becomes a real passion.

I spent my summer therefore amongst the great ones of the earth.

One day we went to a big luncheon-party at the Palace in honour of the birthday of the Emperor Francis Joseph of Austria. It seems strange now to think of having celebrated that event.

Grand Duchess Xenia and the Grand Duke, her husband, came to see my aunt. I admired her charming simplicity, she took a snapshot of my aunt with her son and myself and afterwards sent us each a copy accompanied by a charming little note.

The Grand Duchesses were always dressed as simply as possible, tailor-made dresses and small sailor-hats; so much so, that it really seemed to be a uniform.

These sailor-hats appeared to me as being rather *rétrograde* for the sensible craze for these generally becoming hats had been for some time no longer the fashion in France, and to wear one would have seemed very *démodé*.

That summer Plehve, the Minister, was the victim of a bomb explosion while crossing the bridge opposite the Warsaw station in his carriage, on his way to Peterhof from Petrograd, where he was going to present his usual report to the Tzar ; and this, in spite of the tremendous speed at which the horses were going, for his life was always in danger, as well as that of every one in the government and about the Court at that time. We were to have travelled by the same train and only changed our mind at the last minute.

His death made a great impression, although he was thoroughly detested by all parties, but the Tzar lost in him a strong pillar of autocratic rule. The debris of his carriage were blown up as high as the fourth floor of the neighbouring houses, and this explosion caused the death of, at least, twenty other persons—the unfortunate Minister being literally blown to atoms and the assassin himself injured.

A young and charming officer whom my aunt knew very well was killed ; and another friend of hers whilst driving in his carriage 100 yards away from the scene of the outrage was dazed by the explosion, the coachman falling on to his lap and the horse being thrown down. Another officer became deaf, so terrific was the report of the bursting of the infernal machine.

A few minutes later we passed the actual spot on our way to the station, and saw the remains of the late Minister's carriage strewn all over the road.

Witte succeeded Plehve ; he had the reputation of being clever and strong but also of being

THE FULFILMENT OF MY DREAM

utterly unscrupulous and untrustworthy. He was sent to America to discuss the peace terms of the Russo-Japanese war. Nearly every one thought he was not a man to fulfil such an important mission, for he inspired very little confidence. However, on his return, he was made a Count. He was a friend of the Kaiser and demonstrated this feeling too well before his end.

On Sundays I sometimes went to Mass at Cronstadt, the great naval fortress which should protect Petrograd from an attack by sea—may it now make good its *raison d'être*! is my most humble prayer, October 26th, 1917—in a very fine steamer which only took half an hour to do the crossing from the mainland, and was always crowded with people and laden with horses and carriages.

Cronstadt is by no means a pretty town in spite of its wide streets, and evidently the City Fathers were not a very energetic body as the walls of the theatre which was completely gutted by fire thirty years previously were still standing in their ruined state, while some of the actual panes of glass were still to be seen in their broken window frames, flapping in the wind.

The Catholic church is very large. I noticed how many of the shops bore French and German names, and not merely German names but also a great number of inscriptions, denoting particular wares, Cronstadt being a very commercial city and probably seething with German spies.

The place has distinguished itself lately by establishing itself as a separate Republic with the notorious Lenin as president—which state of affairs, however, was short lived.

A somewhat curious feature in certain places is that the pavements, instead of being composed of flags of stone or brick, are made of small pierced iron squares. The great solemn masses of the men-of-war lying at anchor in the harbour seemed to be sleeping on the still waters—unconscious as yet of the fearful doom that awaited so many of them in the Sea of Japan.

I was interested watching a young naval officer from a pinnace trying to conceal from public view beneath his cloak a superb bouquet of bright red flowers, evidently the symbol of the very ardent love he bore ashore.

The sentinels apparently considered I was too long stationary in one place, as they began to look me up and down with suspicion, which amused me very much.

A lovely walk bordered by a number of weeping willows runs for a long distance by the sea into which they dip their branches.

At that time, there was living at Cronstadt an Orthodox priest, Father John of Cronstadt. He possessed a great personality, and was very well known in Russia. People, in some instances, positively worshipped him, giving him a reputation for working miracles, also of being a very holy man and even a prophet.

Once I ran after a war hero and pulled him by

THE FULFILMENT OF MY DREAM

his sleeve, whereupon he turned round and gave me such a saucy look! But, showing my photographic apparatus, I made him understand that I only wanted to take his photograph. He beamed all over and I placed next to him another hero. They were both survivors of the glorious *Koreitz* which not long before perished in the fatal Sea of Japan.

Then, I was told of a church which was nearer to us; so one Sunday I determined to go there, but, to my horror, I suddenly found myself in the courtyard of some military barracks where there was a chapel—but not mine!

There I was, I and my *coucouchka* or little cab, surrounded by a double row of soldier giants, but luckily being able to mutter a few words in Russian a friendly policeman put me on the right road.

We flew along, passing woods, bridges, and a large palace which was used for the Red Cross work.

I was told that the preceding winter, at The Hermitage, where the Empress often came to work, she had a nigger who helped her to pull out the bastings from her sewing.

At last I arrived at my destination and driving up to a charming little church saw advancing towards me a smart-looking officer, a great friend of Uncle Cherwachidze, Count Beckendorff, brother of the late Russian Ambassador in London, and holding an important post at Court. He was carrying an enormous prayerbook, almost as big as himself.

I went several times to the races at Crasnoë-Celo, which I will refrain from giving a description of, as Count Tolstoi's account in his marvellous novel, *Anna Karenina*, gives one the best idea of this exclusively military meeting.

CHAPTER V

GREAT preparations now began for the baptism of the Tzarevitch. I shall never forget with what joy we heard the appointed number of guns fired announcing the glad tidings that a son and heir had been born to the Emperor and Empress.

This happy event—July 30th, 1904—coincided with the Silver Wedding day of my uncle and aunt, my aunt being the recipient of many beautiful and valuable gifts from the Empress-Dowager, Grand Duchess Xenia and many others. My Uncle Cherwachidze presented me with a charming curbed chain Faberge bangle made of the three golds, as the Russians say, namely of white gold or platinum, red gold and green gold. It was a delicate attention on his part and one, which needless to say, I greatly appreciated.

Since the birth of his son, the Emperor appeared radiant.

I saw him shortly after the event at Crasnoë-Celo races distributing the prizes amongst the winners from the Imperial stand, which resembles a small villa with a balcony on the first floor—as is customary in Russian houses.

Then I saw Grand Duke Cyril, just back from the war in Manchuria where he had fallen into a hole ; he was recuperating and declared that the air of Petrograd was the only one that could improve his health !

He was at this time paying attention to his divorced cousin, whom he eventually married in spite of the Tzar's disapproval.

We went also to the Tzaria, the great national festival, and were invited to the Imperial tent ; the Empress-Dowager drove up in a carriage with four horses and postilions. The Court uniforms were most brilliant. My uncle appeared again all in gold lace. The scene was most beautiful and impressive.

For the baptism of Grand Duke Alexis, heir to the throne, we first went to the Countesses Koutousoff, two sisters, maids of honour to the Empress-Dowager, where we found Countess Worontsoff and the others in full Russian Court Dress, of dark green velvet, as she was mistress of the Court of the Empress-Dowager, each Grand Duke's Court having its own particular colour.

There we met a number of friends, amongst whom were a Princess Troubetzkoy and her husband, and Princess Yousoupoff, a great friend of my aunt. The latter was absolutely charming, I thought, so pretty and so simple. She possesses the largest fortune in Russia, and jewels —such as one reads of in fairy tales.

Her second son was there, who notwithstanding a rather effeminate appearance has distinguished himself lately by being implicated in the murder of that arch-fiend and mock monk Rasputin.

Very soon after the baptism of Grand Duke

THE FULFILMENT OF MY DREAM

Alexis, the eldest son was killed in a duel; he had fallen head over ears in love with a well-known girl in Russian Society, but his parents absolutely refused to sanction this alliance. In consideration of their position and of their immense fortune, they imagined that the only suitable wife for their son must be the daughter of a Grand Duke.

Accordingly, the announcement of the young lady's engagement to another suitor was made public and the religious ceremony took place in Paris, but that very night she gave her husband the slip and flew to the hotel where her lover awaited her.

The result of this naturally was a duel in which the lover was killed by the husband—his dead body being sent back to his home quite unattended in his motor—and some time after his adversary became mad.

Petrograd society was dumbfounded by this drama and for many years the young woman who was the cause of it was looked at askance, but now, I have heard, she is being readmitted into the enchanted circle.

Prince and Princess Yousoupoff were quite overcome with sorrow and could not reconcile themselves to the fact that they would never see their adored son again. They had his body embalmed and laid in a glass coffin, so that they could gaze upon his features, and made a point of conveying the coffin with them wherever they went. This state of things went on for over a year, until one day a friend broke it quietly to them that it was high time to put the coffin out of sight ; and this they finally agreed to do.

The Yousoupoffs' second and only remaining son has accomplished the feat of marrying the beautiful sister of Grand Duke Dmitri, thus satisfying his parents' ambition, and should be universally applauded for having helped to rid Russia and the whole world of that most evil genius of the age, the mock monk Rasputin, who through his deplorable influence over the pro-German Empress Alexandra Feodorovna has been the cause not only of the fall of the House of Romanoff and of that supremely brilliant Court but also, I fear, of the complete downfall of great Holy Russia—at least for generations to come.

The Imperial *cortège* was truly fairy-like : there were gilt coaches surmounted at the four corners by white ostrich feathers, drawn by four or eight white horses with white harness and white plumes on their heads ; the bridle of each horse being held by a footman dressed in white and gold.

In one of the coaches was Princess Galitzine, Grand Mistress of the Court, and in her arms the then precious infant, a very fine child, with blue eyes and dark hair.

The religious ceremony in the Imperial Chapel was indescribably beautiful. I fancied myself in Fairyland. My aunt was of course in full Court dress and looked a real picture in her velvet dress with a lot of her jewels on her *kakochnik* or head-dress.

THE FULFILMENT OF MY DREAM

About this cradle surrounded as it was by so much love—and also by so much hate, during these already troublous times—one could not help but ask oneself, with anxious feelings at the bottom of one's heart, as to what the future held in store for this innocent babe, born in the purple : the hope of the Romanoffs—the target of its enemies.

Prince Dolgorouky, who was Gold Stick in Waiting, drove past in a gilded open state carriage looking the regular *grand seigneur* with his air of supreme distinction as he held his long wand of office in his right hand. In spite of his already advanced age and of his silvery locks, he was still a superb-looking man. One unwelcome shower having fallen during the return journey rather damaged the splendour of his white plumed hat and splendid uniform.

I knew all the members of his family very well, as they and the Nicolays were on very intimate terms with one another. His sister, Madame d'Albédinsky, had been a great friend of the Emperor Alexander III. She was charming—most sympathetic.

A few days later we attended the parade of the Chevaliers-Gardes at Peterhof ; a magnificent spectacle, the troops wearing white uniforms with silver helmets surmounted by a golden eagle with outspread wings.

On one side a carpet had been laid down and priests were offering up prayer, for there is never any ceremony in Russia without a religious side to it.

I often met Baron Fredericks—since then he has become Count—who had been Grand Marshal of the Court for many years. He was to be seen here, there, and everywhere and must have proved himself a most useful spy of the Kaiser— as recent events have indicated.

On the outbreak of the late Revolution he was found in hiding and promptly imprisoned in the Fortress of St Peter and St Paul; from which, however, in consideration of his great age and for a big lump sum of money he has been released.

Princess Lise Bagration-Moucransky, my aunt's friend, was on intimate terms with all the crowned heads and even the non-crowned ones of the Imperial family. One day I went with her to see Grand Duke Michael-Michaelovitch and his daughter, Grand Duchess of Mecklenburg-Schwerin—of whom I shall have more to say later on.

I found the Princess quite charming; " elle avait dû avoir beaucoup de ' chien,' " as we say in France, and still had a very merry twinkle in her eye which caused me great amusement. Being a Bagration, she was descended from the Royal House of Georgia, and her husband—who had been dead some years—had held numerous high appointments.

One day I went with my aunt to see Grand Duchess of Oldenburg, sister of the Tzar—who has since divorced the Grand Duke, to marry his aide-de-camp—she lived quite near us; also Grand Duke and Duchess of Leuchtenbergh.

THE FULFILMENT OF MY DREAM 49

This corner of the world seemed to be peopled with nothing but Royalties !

One of our frequent visitors was a very dignified and decided though kind looking cousin of my uncle's, also a Princess Cherwachidze, who was maid of honour to Grand Duchess Eugénie of Oldenburg.

It pleased my uncle sometimes to be extremely gay and amusing, and I remember what fun we had together singing " Viens, Poupoule, viens." This was then a favourite refrain of the Paris Boulevards, which the Russians adored.

There were at Oranienbaum, near Peterhof, a great number of soldiers getting ready to start for the theatre of war, wearing caps covered with a sort of greenish grey cloth and blouses of the same shade, with khaki coloured greatcoats, which they always wore. The officers wore green tunics and dark caps.

One evening at six o'clock we went to see them take their departure and I never shall forget the beauty of the setting for that sad scene—the Baltic seemed to have borrowed something of the deep warm tones of the Mediterranean. Cronstadt stood out, in the distance across the water, as clear against the radiantly blue sky as if it had been painted for some stage scenery.

There they were, bands playing and flags waving in the breeze, all those gallant fellows having mustered from many different parts of the Empire, all ready to step into that long brick-red train with the Imperial Arms emblazoned on it, which would convey them far, far away to other Steppes, but desert ones these —and terrible.

How many restrained tears in those dark or blue eyes, to which pain and suffering had given an almost terrible expression, and how many never to be realized dreams were enclosed behind these broad foreheads. How melancholy—sad, too—were the expressions on the fresh faces of the young, as on the wrinkled ones of the old peasant women with their heads almost entirely concealed beneath wide gaudy coloured handkerchiefs.

From time to time the stillness of this great pathetic scene was disturbed by the shrill and joyous tones of a voice of a child too young as yet to understand the true and awful significance of this—for many—the last earthly farewell. How numerous they were—these poor little innocents!

When the bell announcing the starting of the train rang for the third time, one last and long hurrah was raised by the entire sad-hearted multitude; and it was terrible to think of the hardships those poor fellows would be subjected to during that long journey to accomplish across Siberia, forty of them in one truck, an open one very often!

Ammunition and guns were conveyed by the same train, which I was told would take six weeks to reach its destination. Altogether a most poignant spectacle, which greatly impressed me; but nowadays such an event as the one I

THE FULFILMENT OF MY DREAM 51

have attempted to describe has become, alas, a common occurrence in almost every country of the world which is traversing the most terrible agony of pain and sorrow of all time.

The Emperor had come and bid them farewell the night before.

As Oranienbaum is so near Cronstadt, it was a favourite place for the wives of sailors with their, usually, large families to live in.

Amongst my aunt's numerous men-servants there was one called Coucoulsky who was the head butler—very fat and rotund, with the usual flat head of the Pole, wearing enormous whiskers, with a pair of tiny sparkling eyes always filled with astonishment. The poor man was no longer young—il sue, il souffle, il est rendu—and to put him into this state it was merely sufficient for him to offer to his little Princess on a huge silver tray some wonderful *pièce montée*, which he held at such an angle that one always expected to see the contents flung into her lap. This he did with a most beatified expression on his broad smiling face.

He was for ever tripping up over imaginary obstacles, and always appeared to be running, but somehow or other he never managed to be there when required; this was inexplicable. And yet, in this fanciful and fantastic being, there was a soul, an exquisite poetic soul.

In the summer on moonlight nights, afar off in the garden, alone amongst the shrubs, his comical profile could be seen detaching itself against the sky, his huge mouth wide open, his whiskers trembling and his little eyes closed; while he sang languorously. Three fox terriers disturbed in their slumbers by these nocturnal sounds always made a combined attack on him, threatening to bite his calves to the bone. One by one the windows of the house were closed, but all in vain—nothing could distract him from this reverie of song!

One evening, on one of the rare occasions of a visit from Prince Cherwachidze, Coucoulsky appeared with a radiant expression carrying a *plat monté,* as my amorous little aunt was determined to welcome her spouse by setting before him a regular feast.

Every one's surprise was great on perceiving the faithful butler with a napkin like a child's immense bib tied beneath his chin, he in his anxiety having forgotten to remove it and no one venturing to remind him of its existence as neither my aunt, on account of her short sightedness, nor my uncle, owing to his usual state of oblivion, had noticed the grotesque appearance of the poor man, as he trotted and scrambled round the table balancing the huge dish and threatening everybody with a douche of its contents.

Later on, I found out that the reason for his wearing the bib was on account of the desire to preserve the freshness of his highly-starched collar when off duty—but on this celebrated occasion he had forgotten to remove it.

Although the charms of poor Coucoulsky were many, my aunt failed to see them in their true

THE FULFILMENT OF MY DREAM

light and, after a few months, he with many tears of regret was obliged to leave this hospitable interior where he was considered both too old and too young. He left but too few regrets, only the memory of him made many laugh.

He was quite unique, this good Coucoulsky. He returned to his wife who was somewhat old, rather ugly and with only one eye, but to him she appeared always full of charm and grace—she never was more beautiful nor less blind—but they were young, both of them. Oh, the good old time!

CHAPTER VI

LIFE at Michaelovka was very gay and delightful, in that beautiful palace belonging to Grand Duke Michael-Michaelovitch on the shore of the Baltic, and surrounded by every possible luxury amidst a gay and numerous suite.

Michaelovka is situated at Strelna, quite near Peterhof. I stayed there with my uncle, General de Baranoff, and my aunt. My uncle was Grand Marshal of the Court of Grand Duke Michael-Michaelovitch, who always spent a great part of each summer there.

The poor Grand Duke Michael-Michaelovitch was then very old and in failing health and was not often visible—for years past he had spent his winters at Cannes, where he owned the beautiful Villa Kasbeck.

My uncle and aunt made a perfect couple and ideal parents. It was a genuine pleasure for one to see their two white heads approach one another several times a day and join in an affectionate embrace. I had met my uncle on the Riviera when at Cannes some years previously and also General Tolstoi, both forming part of the suite of the Grand Duke. General Tolstoi could be really witty at times, and once I remember he amused us greatly when he came

THE FULFILMENT OF MY DREAM 55

to see us with my uncle. Bowing and bending himself with that grace and suppleness peculiar to the Russian he pretended to efface himself while ushering in my uncle and said: " Je vous présente un grand ravageur." Of this particular side of my uncle's character I know nothing, but I can well believe he might have been the cause of many a heart beat, and I for one should have heartily congratulated each one of those hearts for the good taste they showed.

Very tall and thin, very intelligent beneath an impassive countenance, kindness itself, General de Baranoff combines the acme of distinction with the personification of honesty; very fond, like nearly all Russians, of putting questions to foreigners but making a point of never answering any—himself a past master in the art.

Grand Duke Michael-Michaelovitch, however, paid full justice to my uncle's great integrity and appreciated the advantage of having at his side a man of his high character, for they were often surrounded by sycophants of whom, however, one might say that they followed the example of their august masters in that their needs were insatiable and unsatisfied, certainly a thorn in the side of the Imperial crown; so much so that one day while walking with one of my aunts in the palace grounds, we were passed by a big motor-car, salutations were exchanged and I asked my aunt who was the gorgeous occupant.

"C'est le Grand Duc, . . ." she said, " le ' seul ' qui soit sérieux ! "

Unlike the rest of the suite of Grand Duke Michael-Michaelovitch, my uncle never took any advantage of his position and would never even take at the Grand Duke's expense a single trunk with him beyond what was strictly necessary, though he accompanied him on all his journeys— Cannes, Baden-Baden, etc. This was in vivid contrast to one of the Grand Duke's retinue, who never spent a penny except at his master's charge and even went so far as to get the Grand Duke to pay the tickets of all his family and finally persuaded him to rent for them a Villa at Cannes much to the disgust of my uncle. I never liked this person with a German sounding name and a doubtful profile.

I often said to my aunt, "Do you know, I almost entertain a passion for my uncle," whereupon she used to smile that beautiful smile of hers which I liked seeing so much.

My Aunt de Baranoff, *née* de Bibikoff, was charming ; she had beautiful white hair and very pretty blue eyes, and in her youth must have been very much admired.

She combined tremendous entrain with much affability, and in her own set she was what might be called, in schoolboy language, a jolly good sort, which pleased me—her reflections being always to the point, and time spent with her never lagged. How we used to laugh over things together ! I shall always retain much affection for her. I believe her first husband—whom she divorced—was a perfect brute to her.

By her marriage with my uncle she had two children; her daughter Olga was married to Lieutenant de Zinovieff, in the Garde à Cheval quartered at Petrograd, a late page of the Empress, but she was for the time being at the Camp of Crasnoë-Celo, not far from us, and I spent a few delightful days with her.

Russian soldiers always leave their barracks during the summer months and camp out of doors—those of Petrograd going into the neighbourhood. This healthy measure is never practised in France, which is a great mistake I think; and I always admired these huge camps composed of innumerable white tents, like parasols, erected in perfect symmetry, looking from a distance like so many small white mushrooms instead of being the improvised shelters of these giant-like soldiers. The Camp of Crasnoë-Celo was, I think, the largest.

Her son Petia, the regular type of a true Russian, not without charm and dark and good-looking, was at that time preparing at the Lycée to enter the regiment of the Chevaliers-Gardes in which he held a distinguished position before the war.

My poor aunt, fearing the wars, wanted him to choose a diplomatic career, but nothing would induce him to change his mind. He is now in the trenches—or was lately—and has been badly wounded once.

During the summer the heat is at times very

intense in Russia—a kind of damp heat like the mild hot vapours of a conservatory—and the nights on the coast of the Baltic were very damp and a thick white steam rose spirally from the ground in patches, like smoke, between the Palace and the sea, which caused a most curious effect.

My aunt had one daughter, Lily, by her first marriage and she and I became great friends. She also lived with her parents, as she had been obliged to leave a brute of a husband who was an officer of the Lancers of the Guard, of which my uncle was in command at the time of her marriage at Peterhof. Not long after her marriage she had gone away for a few days to visit a relation who was ill, and on her return she found her own house occupied not only by her husband's mistress but by the children of that illicit union as well. The wretch then proposed to her that she should remain on in the house and that they should all live together, which proposition she naturally scorned and thereupon returned to her old home.

She divorced the man in consequence, but not, like most people in Russian society, in order to try her luck again, having already looked out for number " two "—not at all, once having recovered her liberty she took good care to preserve it.

Her library seemed to me to be literally filled with the works of Anatole France and Pierre Loti, and my acquaintance with literature owing to my strict French upbringing being more than limited—I had scarcely ever read anything but fairy tales until then—I consequently found it extremely difficult to talk to our friends with any clear knowledge of those popular French authors about whom I was always being questioned.

Lily seemed to take me somewhat under her wing and gave me—at least in words—an insight into life; and with the passing of time I have often thought how very much to the point her doctrine was.

Colonel Echappard du Breuil was frequently to be seen at my aunt's house, he claimed to be of French origin, his ancestors having escaped—échappé—across the Pyrenées into France at the time of the Moorish expulsion from Spain, during the reign of the " Catholic Kings," Ferdinand and Isabella—hence the origin of this somewhat curious name.

The Colonel was attached to the suite of Grand Duke George, and whenever I asked him where he was going he always replied " To Christophky "—to the grand café-concert, on the island of that name at The Islands—and he never ceased expatiating on the charms of the fair and dark beauties of that delectable spot. He was a jolly fellow with a fat round face wreathed in smiles—he seemed to render the very atmosphere sunny.

And Lily behind the wings—*dans les coulisses*, as we say in France—used to hum to salute his departure the following refrain, which she had taught me and which we loved, this charming little refrain about the three cocks :—

>Cocorico oooo
>Quand je veux, je peux.
>(Le jeune coq.)

>Cocorico oooo
>Quand je peux, je veux.
>(Coq d'âge moyen.)

>Cocorico ooooo
>Que vous êtes heureux.
>(Le vieux coq.)

Oh, how we did pity you, poor old man! And we did not allow feathers to grow in this hen coup, but, willy-nilly, spurs and uniform of some *attaché de la suite*.

Another character was General Tolstoi, whom I have already mentioned. He came very often to see us, especially when we were in Petrograd; he frequently spoke Russian and recounted interminably long stories in that language which I regret to say used to make me yawn, as I could not always follow them, and just to tease me, at the most critical part of the story, he rapidly changed from Russian into French so that my ears should receive the full benefit of it all. *Quel toupet!*

One evening, he told us of how he had once climbed up a tree, and from there had had an uninterrupted view over a high fence, behind which, apparently believing themselves to be sheltered from inquisitive eyes, some members of the fair sex were in the full enjoyment of a sun bath cure! These descendants of Eve were walking about in their birthday costumes, so that the marvellous effects of the luminous rays should have full play. On this occasion his particular attention was drawn to a certain Titianesque beauty.

I pictured him in this attitude looking like a hideous orang-outang squatting on a branch of a tree—as he, poor fellow, was not endowed with any personal beauty!

If I am not mistaken, I am afraid he has since come to a tragic end attributed to debts.

At my Aunt de Baranoff's all the suite of the Grand Duke came more or less every day and Prince Orbeliani with them, always shuffling his feet on the floor and making a terrible noise in doing so; this unfortunate peculiarity, apart from being an illness from which nearly all the members of his family suffer, was with him to some extent a pose—où va-t-elle se nicher—la pose!—and a very disturbing one, too, as far as I was concerned.

As luck would have it, the princely apartments were situated just over my bedroom, so that every morning my peaceful slumbers were disturbed by his Excellency's shufflings, which he admitted he accentuated just to tease me.

He was married to Countess Kleinmichel, the daughter of old Countess Kleinmichel who entertained a good deal in Petrograd; the latter had the reputation of being a spy for Germany, and was arrested at the outbreak of the Revolution; she was also it appears a fervent sister disciple of Rasputin's new religion.

Princess Lobanoff was another frequent guest at my aunt's, she was maid of honour to Grand Duchess George, and was so imbued with the sense of her own importance that she could not even cross the courtyard of the palace on foot and always had her carriage ordered for the transit.

She finally married an American who lives in California. What must be her impression of that democratic country, I wonder? But what would she feel like being in Russia now! The sister of Princess Lobanoff had married an Englishman, Sir Edwin Egerton, then Minister at Athens; he was much older than his wife.

Grand Duchess George is a Greek princess, sister of the ex-King Tino. She did not look very pleasant I thought. She was very fond of riding.

One day my Aunt de Baranoff and I were invited to tea by a friend, a lieutenant of the Cossacks of the Guard—Cossacks of the Escort. This was a very select corps, always in attendance on the Emperor, and a very picked body of men they were, with their wild expressions and wasp-like waists.

The Cossacks are extraordinarily active and supple, with their soft leather boots which pull on like stockings and have no hard soles. Our young host was a great favourite of the Grand Duchesses at Court Balls, as he danced very well. He ordered his men to sing and dance

CRONSTADT—TWO SURVIVORS OF THE GLORIOUS KOREITZ

THE BARRACKS AT PETERHOF, TWO COSSACKS OF THE ESCORT

THE CROWN PRINCE OF GERMANY WITH PRINCESS CECILIE
AS FIANCÉS

THE FULFILMENT OF MY DREAM 63

for us, which performance I greatly enjoyed, especially the sword dance. Their horses seem to possess quite a special intelligence and to have been circus trained. I took photographs of the company in their Peterhof barracks and later sent a copy to each member.

Grand Duchess Anastasia of Mecklenburg-Schwerin, daughter of Grand Duke Michael-Michaelovitch, was also spending her summer at Michaelovka. She often invited my aunt to dinner, but these invitations to help to amuse " Satanasia "—as she is nicknamed in Germany —were sometimes a doubtful pleasure even to my aunt, as the task must have been a difficult one at times.

Grand Duchess Anastasia was no longer what is called a " young " woman, but she had a beautiful figure and was very striking-looking. She, too, affected the wearing of sailor-hats— and thick white veils!

Princess Cecilie, her daughter, was very attached to my young cousin Olga and often came to tea with us. The German Crown Prince and she had met at the same house previously and had become almost secretly engaged, as there were difficulties in the way of their union. The Kaiser was against the marriage, but the young people met again the following winter at Cannes—this, in spite of furious messages from the War Lord recalling his son to Germany, but the Crown Prince paid no heed to them, so it is related. It is also told by people who met the fiancés on the Riviera that their eyes were sometimes swollen by tears shed because of the Emperor's resistance, which was caused by his dislike of Grand Duchess Anastasia, whom he always refused to receive at Court since the marriage.

Although Princess Cecilie is not as handsome as her mother, yet she is tall and graceful and most attractive.

The vision of a throne must have had a great deal to do with her choice, I fancy; and she was reputed to have said that she would only consent to marry a " throne " !

At the Russian Court it was rather expected that she might have married the Tzar's brother, but he never paid her any attention, and she declared to her lady-in-waiting that there were too many bombs in Russia and that she no longer wished to remain there !

One of the favourite games of Grand Duke Michael-Alexandrovitch, the Tzar's brother and at that time his heir, was to place a potato in a pail of water and then get his friends down on all fours to lean over the pail and with their mouths try to extract the wretched thing—usually with such results as might be imagined, some clumsy jaws sinking so deep into the water as almost to cause their owner's death by drowning, while the potato seemed to take pleasure in their discomfiture by rising and sinking at every touch to a most alarming degree.

Another visitor staying at the Palace was Prince Cristopher of Greece, brother of ex-King Tino and of Grand Duchess George, who always

THE FULFILMENT OF MY DREAM

came with Princess Cecilie to see my aunt. He was a fat boy of about fourteen at the time and full of every conceivable mischief. One of his greatest jokes was to leap with both feet into the middle of a mud puddle so as to splash the Princess and my cousin from head to foot !

My aunt remarked to him once in front of me that he seemed to be very fond of his cousin—Princess Cecilie—upon which he blushed to the roots of his hair and exclaimed " Moi, je n'aime personne ! "

The following year Princess Cecilie married the German Crown Prince and three weeks after she sent a telegram to my cousin Olga—they have corresponded for years—saying : " Je suis très heureuse." I wonder if she is still of the same opinion !

Now, she has become the mother of a large family, and quite " German " I am told.

She had been brought up very severely by her mother, as is so often the way with parents who are not over-particular concerning their own mode of living.

Grand Duke of Mecklenburg-Schwerin, seemingly unconscious of the charms of his beautiful Villa Wenden at Cannes, of the perfume of the lovely roses and all the other exquisite flowers of his garden, was perhaps preoccupied in another direction of life, which must have been full of heavy storm clouds for him, so heavy indeed that he felt unable to bear them and one day threw himself over the parapet of the bridge in his park which traverses the road—and there was found the dead body of the Grand Duke.

Grand Duchess Anastasia, at Cannes as elsewhere, led a joyous life, and a supposed attack of measles, with an unusual and far-reaching result—not always experienced by those suffering from that complaint—made the whole Riviera talk and most of it smile a little maliciously perhaps.

Her men-servants were chosen for their good looks—and, if rumour said truly, each one of those ran a good chance of promotion; though her private secretary was always supposed to be the most favoured one.

Since I left Russia I have often seen her in Paris.

One day, in far distant Mecklenburg, an aeronaut fell from the heavens into her park. Accidentally or not, he made no mistake and found on terra firma his consolations—good nursing, for he was wounded on descending, and care so tender and true that after several years he was still there. Perhaps he may have accompanied his benefactress to Russia as since the outbreak of war the Grand Duchess returned to her native land, no longer wishing to have anything more to do with Germany and the Kaiser—at least she says so—to whom she owes a great grudge for his harshness.

Lily was again often requested to go to Mecklenburg, to resume her previous occupation of lady-in-waiting to H.I.H.; but this situation was no longer enviable or possible and she politely begged to be excused.

I have heard that Anastasia is in Cannes, on the French Riviera, spending her winters there as before, though not amidst the same gaiety. Last winter she often went to visit a certain military hospital, but was asked to come no more. The Crown Princess actually paid a visit to her mother there last winter, but not officially of course!

Numbers of the secret police invaded the Grand Duke's park, and it seemed to me that one was to be met with at every few yards; but as they knew who I was they did not interfere with me. With their long coats buttoned up at the neck, their dark blue ties, and each carrying a walking stick, their appearance amused me rather in spite of the grave functions imposed upon them.

CHAPTER VII

WHILE I was at Michaelovka the Revolution was gaining ground every day. Russia was going through a critical period of her history and one felt as though one was living on a volcano—yet, in the end, an approximative degree of order came out of what looked like being chaos.

An attempt against the Tzar's life was really to be feared, and during a certain time the railway line from Peterhof to Petrograd by which he often travelled had a military guard, a close cordon of troops being placed below the embankment on which the train passed, on both sides of the track. A bomb there would have done important work as these trains were always conveying Ministers and Grand Dukes.

After dinner we often went to listen to " La Musique Rouge," the Emperor's private band; the musicians were dressed in red, each one of them being an artist. They played in the park at Peterhof, to which we drove in a large open landau and took our place in the long line of carriages there to meet numbers of friends. These concerts, however, were soon after discontinued on account of the growing troubles.

The Empress-Dowager often came over from

THE FULFILMENT OF MY DREAM 69

Peterhof driving herself a low carriage with a pair of black horses and wearing a black sailor-hat!

Another frequent visitor at Michaelovka was a young Count Toll, in the Lancers of the Guard, cousin of my uncle Count Pahlen, and also related by marriage to the late Russian Ambassador in Paris, Monsieur Isvoltzky; and this recalls to my memory an interesting incident which was the direct cause of the latter's advancement.

The father of Madame Isvoltzky, *née* Countess Toll, Russian Minister at Copenhagen, was most anxious to get his daughter suitably married—which seemed rather a difficult task—and informed the Emperor of the situation, who despatched several couriers to Copenhagen with this idea. At last Isvoltzky—whose chief recommendations perhaps were his intelligence and the high favour in which he stood at Court—was sent. On this errand of courtship he was successful, and the Emperor made a career for him. All went well with poor Isvoltzky until the outbreak of the Revolution, when naturally he was amongst the first to be recalled and humbled.

I have often been to their receptions at the Russian Embassy in Paris. He was very clever, but possessed neither the presence nor the exquisite manners of his predecessor, Count de Nelidoff.

The celebration of my Aunt de Baranoff's birthday was a great event: a regular *défilé* of celebrities both civil and military; every regiment seemed to have been represented and the drawing-rooms were more than ever filled with flowers—a regular avalanche in fact.

The dinner-party in the evening was of the gayest. I sat between Colonel Echappard and the Russian Minister at Dresden and was anything but dull.

In Russia birthday anniversaries are always made a great deal of. The heroine of the occasion is always dressed in white or pearl grey and no one is allowed to wear black. Even if one is in mourning, one must discard its outward signs for the day or else keep away from the fête altogether.

I never shall forget the gaiety of those 1 a.m. teas at Michaelovka, the tables being laden with the choicest fruits, melons, strawberries, peaches in abundance, all that Nature could be persuaded to produce. Those mountains of luscious fruit, set in the most tasteful style amidst the richest of table decorations imaginable, would have made a perfect subject for any great artist of still life to reproduce on canvas. These midnight or early morning teas I thought a delightful custom. In Russia the night is turned into day, which fascinated me.

People actually call on one another between 11 p.m. and midnight, and I often accompanied my aunts on such visits; I wonder what sort of a reception nocturnal visitors in hum-drum Western Europe would receive should anyone venture to ring the front bell at that hour: a house plunged in darkness and at every door

THE FULFILMENT OF MY DREAM

a glimpse of pyjama or visions of more diaphanous raiment and, above, angry, sleepy, maybe frightened physiognomies, anxiously inquiring who the intruder was who dared to come at such an hour; and Cerberus would either refuse to answer the door or else give a month's notice from to-morrow!

Then on retiring to my own room I sat down in the white light of the white nights and took up my pen and wrote to far away France; and I am sure the reader will understand what my feelings were on my return to my pacific and unchangeable Normandy, when I had to rejoin Morpheus at 10 p.m.

From time to time Petia, whom I always called "the dear little cousin," used to take his sister Olga, who was often there, and me out in a little Canadian canoe, which certainly looked a most fragile craft; and one day, whilst contemplating the two birthday suits of nymphs who were bathing not far away—this being the custom it appears in summer time—I had visions which were almost realized of being upset into the water and having to save ourselves by hanging on to a bunch of bulrushes. Olga and I got off safely, however; but I decided never more to follow the nymph-lover again on the still waters of the Gulf.

My attention was often drawn to a certain monk in the streets of Peterhof, carrying a long iron staff in his hand. His hair—which he wore very long—was of reddish colour, his eyes had a haggard expression and his complexion was burnt and bronzed by continual exposure to the sun and to that " vent de Russie " of which Pierre Loti always speaks in his books. This striking and unusual figure was dressed in a rather short white habit. I am almost certain I saw him once or twice again, years after, in the Champs-Élysées in Paris. He belonged to a Greek orthodox sect who walk from place to place the whole year round living on charity, they are called *staretz*. He must doubtless have walked there by slow stages right across Europe as the pilgrims of old were wont to do.

Amongst the many people who came to see my aunt at Michaelovka I have forgotten to mention an old Baron Winspear who was charming; although he was a Neapolitan, he had made all his career at the Court of Grand Duke Michael-Michaelovitch. Many young aides-de-camp came in relays to do their wait from time to time, amongst them being one who was extraordinarily good-looking.

My uncle used to tease me about him by saying " Il est beau, très beau, Renée," from the height of his impassible face—I use the word height because he is so tall and so straight—and this was said not only once but each time he left the room until it became really a perfect plague ! He certainly was very good-looking, especially when wearing all his decorations, but I never lost my heart to Adonis, who is always so impressed by his own importance that he makes one positively " pant " for *plus de laideur* ; and, besides, he could not speak a word of French.

THE FULFILMENT OF MY DREAM

On this subject I may say that the preceding generation spoke French much better than my generation. French which had been for such a long time the language used at Court, and resorted to in many families, had lost ground and had of late years been dethroned by Russian; consequently many young men spoke it badly.

English since the marriage of Nicholas II. had been much spoken in Court circles. I really wonder why it was not German !

In drawing-rooms one frequently heard four languages spoken at the same time, people passing from one to the other with the utmost facility.

The Russian certainly has the gift of languages; which is a real gift and possesses great charm.

One day I was taken by my aunt to a large monastery situated not very far from Michaelovka. The monks were very *typiques* in their white habits, but I thought to myself I would not care to meet one of them in the dark !

The service was extremely beautiful, as is usually the case in the Greek Church; these services always appeal to me, and it was ever my wont during my travels to attend them as often as I could. That peculiar Russian chant seems to carry one away into another world—a dream world full of mystic ideals. It was on one of these occasions that I witnessed for the first time little babies in their mothers' or nurses' arms having the Blessed Sacrament administered to them; and what astonished me so tremendously was the goodness of these little innocent creatures as they unconsciously went through this great and solemn act. I found this ceremony both touching and pretty; it is a pity the Catholic Church has abandoned its usage.

The Saint-Pairs and I had then intended going to spend a week or two at Stockholm and I was enchanted with the idea; but at the eleventh hour Monsieur Pelletan, then the French Ministre de la Marine—one always wondered the why and wherefore of that appointment, as I am sure, with many others, he had never seen salt water any more than its fresh substitute—refused to allow Monsieur de Saint-Pair on account of his official position at the Embassy to leave his post, owing to the serious political events that were occurring at that time. I was therefore obliged to have my luggage brought back from Petrograd, where it was all ready to be put on board the steamer, feeling rather dejected at having to do so, as we were the bearers of so many charming introductions to all the accredited Ministers and different Members of the Court Circle; and it would have been a real delight to have seen the Venice of the North under such agreeable conditions, while the crossing would only have taken about eighteen hours.

Then I returned to Finland—back again to that enchanting Monrepos, perhaps even more dreamlike than before beneath its exquisite autumn tints. The pretty Isle of Ludwinstein seemed to me more poetic than ever beneath the

THE FULFILMENT OF MY DREAM 75

slow rain of its golden leaves—poignant and lifelike image of the lives which had been but were no more, resting there so near in the depths of the cold sepulchre. The dream of all this Northern Nature enfolded me more closely now than before; in this country where the sun sinks to rest in all the glory of its opalescent rays, in all this translucency of nature which is not shared by us, but belongs entirely to it and seemingly admits us a little way into the abstract world of souls who are no more—but who watch—and everywhere I encountered the shadow of my adored and adoring grandmother.

One Sunday morning on my return from Viborg I perceived some pretty flags composed of bright colours floating in the wind in the clear atmosphere of a most beautiful day. The primitive music had just ceased, and an orator mounted on an upturned barrel was addressing in a loud voice an audience composed of about fifty people. Then I clearly understood, on perceiving the busy bee-like movements of the little poked bonnets all around, the significance of this gathering: it was the Salvation Army to whom my uncle had given permission to hold the meeting in his park.

The effect of this assemblage was pretty beneath the thick dome of pine branches, with long hanging cones through which the rich indigo sky was accentuated in its depths.

We took up boating trips again on the Gulf, going thus very often to Viborg. I envied the faithful Kousma who with my aunt's horses always did the journey to Petrograd from Finland on a ferry-boat, peacefully gliding on the surface of the waves without a thought or care —his soul was pure, he never missed any of the necessary ablutions prescribed by the Prophet; he was a good servant, a true and tender husband —with this enchanting panorama for his eyes to look upon, where the only missing link to perfect bliss for him was the absence of his Mahomet.

At this visit I met my aunt's sister, Countess Czapska. Her property was in the neighbourhood of Cracow, where she also spent a part of the year.

When that part of the country came into the war zone, she sought refuge at Monrepos—but returned to die. She was a charming character, very well read, and combined good will with a great sense of humour.

In the household of my Aunt de Nicolay there was a most important institution whom I ought to have mentioned before, so long had she been there. Mademoiselle Stirry was her name. The usual charms of her sex she lacked entirely. She was as flat as a pancake, all shrunken and crooked, with a few spare hairs growing on her head drawn back with the utmost difficulty on to the skull where they lay spread out; on her cheeks were several beauty spots from which hairs grew in abundance, so large indeed were they that they became hideous by force of their importance; her small eyes were sharp as gimlets and took notice of every one and every-

THE FULFILMENT OF MY DREAM 77

thing, letting nothing escape them, as they gave animation to her most hideous physiognomy with its livid and earthy complexion and, I must not forget, rather important whiskers and beard. Two large square sinewy hands with enormous knuckles, more like a labourer's than the hands of a woman, were attached to a pair of arms far too long for her height and too short for any ordinarily proportioned person. This is a true description of this most faithful and devoted creature of Aline : she performed her duties of housekeeper to the utmost perfection.

She could be positively ferocious at times when anyone ventured to criticize or attack the acts of her mistress ; at others she could be gentle and kind, and fortunately for me I only know her in this light, but could not in spite of this find her beautiful. To be in her good graces was absolutely necessary for every one in the house, otherwise she would make their lives unbearable. Her influence and power were great, and I often thought she sometimes usurped her rights in regard to my aunt.

I am indebted to her, however, for my knowledge of Russian, as she used to give me a lesson in that language every evening when I was in Finland.

One day she announced with great excitement and most mysteriously her intention of spending a few days in Petrograd in order to see a friend of hers—a certain Armenian doctor who was passing through the capital. Before I had caught sight of his dark bearded appearance, and he had rather alarmed me. But love is sometimes blind, isn't it ?

We had much diversion over what we called " les écarts de Mademoiselle Stirry."

" I am sure she is a man in disguise," my Aunt de Baranoff always said. " Look how devotedly attached she is to Aline. Don't you think she must be ? "

I answered laughing that I knew nothing of that and would not possibly allow such an infamous idea to exist.

Aunt Aline possessed a marvellous gift for languages and spoke I don't know how many ; amongst them were Swedish and Finnish, the latter a very difficult language.

Part II
IN THE CAUCASUS

CHAPTER VIII

THE following autumn proved a veritable time of enchantment for me. I spent it in the Caucasus, at Tiflis, with my good and kind aunt, Princess Cherwachidze, who owns a beautiful palace there. I specially admired its large white marble staircase. She also had a beautiful property near Soukhoum, called "Béthanie," not very far from Tiflis, but in consequence of the disturbances at that time we were unable to go there.

Her father, Baron Alexandre de Nicolay, had been the most popular Governor of the Caucasus, where he left behind him a remembrance only equal to that of a dearly loved sovereign; besides this, my aunt is closely allied to all the chief princely families of Georgia—many of them of royal blood. Thus my visit was carried out under the most favourable conditions.

We again met there old Princess Bagration Moucransky, a great personality everywhere, and more especially at Tiflis. She had a beautiful palace and I thought her drawing-rooms very French. She was one of our frequent visitors and we dined at each other's houses constantly. At my aunt's and also at

Princess Moucransky's I met—at least four or five times a week— Prince Louis Napoléon, brother of Prince Victor Napoléon, heir to the Imperial throne of France, and a great friend of my aunt's.

The Prince did not appear often in society, but made exceptions sometimes. The reason for this aloofness was caused by the fixed idea of many Princesses to marry him; one of whom had even gone so far as to be on the point of divorcing her good, thorough-going husband with a view to accomplishing this great feat—and the only missing point in the situation was the consent of Prince Louis himself. So, to avenge themselves on the Prince, the embittered females cried out from the housetops the great news that he was already much married in Tiflis, in a very different milieu to theirs and that he was the father of many little " Bonapartes de la main gauche."

He was in command of several Caucasian regiments and was quartered at Tiflis. I greatly admired his military bearing. At that time he was in despair at not having obtained a command in Manchuria, but it was said that the French Government, fearing that he might gain his laurels there, had petitioned the Russian Government not to send him as he was a general in the Russian Army; Russia, being desirous of keeping on good terms with her French Ally, naturally acquiesced in this request.

IN THE CAUCASUS

I quite understood what the bitterness of his innermost feelings must have been. I often had long and interesting conversations with the Prince which helped me on the banks of the Koura to remember distant France.

One night I went to a Russian play at the theatre with my aunt; and the Prince, who sat next to me, whispered in my ear its version in French. Between the acts he escorted me on his arm to the foyer, when I asked him:

"Monseigneur, et la France? N'y songez-vous donc jamais?"

He looked at me and smiled, then said:

"It would be necessary to change the whole of the Army and the whole of the Navy."

When I told him of the spark of light, still visible very often amongst the Norman peasants of another generation, in the pupils of the old men's eyes, those who had fought the wars of the Empire and would have willingly laid down their lives for their Emperor—whose children now are fighting for France.

The Prince seemed pleased and surprised.

"En tous les cas," me dit-il, "ce ne serait pas à moi mais à mon frère."

As every one knows, his brother Prince Victor Napoléon lived in Brussels and married Princess Clémentine, daughter of the late King of the Belgians, after the death of the latter who for years had been opposed to the marriage. The Prince and Princess have now a daughter and a son and, perhaps, one recalls to memory the touching thought of Princess Clémentine, who when hoping she was going to have a son had some earth brought from France so that the infant, although in exile, might be born on French soil.

He signed his name in my autograph book simply "Louis Napoléon." I should have liked him to have written more but he declined, saying: "It would be commented upon," and that was the reason for his refusal. He told me he would be forty in a few days' time.

He paid long visits to my aunt lasting often more than two hours; she had known him for a long time and had made many things easier for him. In Russia he enjoyed the privileges of a Grand Duke and was treated as such at Court; but as he was not really a Grand Duke many of his brother officers were madly jealous at seeing him already enjoying such an important position and rank which would only be accorded to them when their heads were bald and their joints stiffened by the service and toil of years—if ever!

Luckily for us we had arrived in the Caucasus comparatively fresh after four nights in the train; Russian trains are not so fast as ours and in consequence not so tiring.

My introduction to Princess Orbeliani was, to say the least of it, original in the extreme. I found my hostess with all the other ladies in the room lying face downward on the floor, while the gentlemen of the party stood contemplating with more or less knowledge the somewhat uneven surfaces before them; the rotundity of the female sex is not rare and is much admired in the Caucasus.

The beauty of the average Caucasian woman is by no means a negligible quantity, the type being usually dark with large black eyes; but they grow old prematurely, often becoming very fat. The men are usually tall with wasp-like waists; their features are good, but their expression is very often decidedly savage.

In the mountain districts there exists a fair ruddy type amongst some of the tribes; the women are very pretty and are much admired.

It was subsequently explained to me that these ladies on the floor were really practising a Russian dance and they were taking the parts which should have been allotted to their male partners.

I often met Princess Murat, *née* Princess de Mingrélie, and her daughter Antoinette; her eldest son Lucien had married a daughter of my cousin the late Duc de Rohan, to whom the lovely Castle of Jocelyn in Brittany belongs, while her second son Napoléon, generally called Napo, was fighting on the side of the Russians at the war.

Her daughter Antoinette was looking after her mother's vast estates with the knowledge of a man — and although not dressed in khaki could have shown some of our present-day girls on the land what real hard work means.

Some years previously the Duchesse de Rohan had, much to every one's surprise, married her daughter to Prince Murat, whose ancestors do not date farther back than Napoléon, while the Rohans' motto for generations has been: " Roy ne puis, Prince ne daigne, Rohan suis."

Amongst the three daughters of the Duchess were Princess Talleyrand-Périgord, whose marriage was a failure, but who is dead now. Princess Murat does not get on very well with her husband, so no one was surprised when the third daughter, before selecting a fiancé, exclaimed : " My eldest sister was married to a man who says, ' Vive le Roi,' my other sister to one who says ' Vive l'Empereur,' I want a husband who says ' Vive la Raison.' " She eventually married a Caraman-Chimay.

The various regiments from the basis of all social activity and I spent delightful moments with Princesses Orbeliani, Ratieff, Melikoff, Heristoff, etc. I saw much of the Princess de Georgia and the young Troubetzkoy princes, Nikita and Petia, all more or less related to my aunt; they gave delightful evening parties and I really think I did not spend one evening at home.

The evening parties at Tiflis were of the

IN THE CAUCASUS

gayest, and there was an uninterrupted succession of them. One ended by knowing each other well, as one was continually meeting the same people which I thought was delightful. I saw not a few little glasses of vodka emptied by the gentlemen, but without traces of injurious or disastrous results—" Honi soit qui mal y pense "—with the exception, however, of an old general whose nose was always like a lighthouse, and who I saw fall down three times in the same evening, so tipsy was he; but he was set up again on his legs the same number of times and there was no more to be said. I always found in that liquid an awful smell of methylated spirit and took good care not to get further acquainted with it.

When short of vodka the moujik easily drinks methylated spirit, it appears, and gets drunk on it; this often happened during the last Revolution. And to think that the " Little Father " suppressed the use of it among his troops since the war! What a marvellous result of the so much abused " autocratic " power.

We often began our evenings at the theatre. The Opera was very good; and the house a very fine one; my aunt had her box, needless to say. It was there that I saw performed " Mademoiselle Fifi," that story of Maupassant's, episode of the war of 1870 and 1871 which would, alas, be so life-like to-day. Then we went to visit some of our friends. I must mention a charming party given by an attractive woman à l'air gamin Madame Cheremetieff —Lise. The drawing-rooms represented a little country inn and its garden, what the Italians would describe as an "*osteria.*" It was full of local colour. Round the tables the women in full toilette, most of the men officers in uniform — which the Russians always wear. Many among them officers in the Cossacks and Tcherkesses, wearing on their heads their high astrakhan caps either white or black. Certainly in the soft veiled light it was a very pretty sight, and created a most charming and picturesque effect.

Madame Z——, a rich Armenian, gave charming fêtes, to which my aunt and I often went: excellent *buffet*, amidst every possible luxury. But the story of this lady having been discovered in her own house a few days before on the knees of a young officer, whose moustache she was lovingly pulling, somewhat cooled my aunt's feelings towards her and she begged me not to go there without her in the future.

Anyone of importance passing through Tiflis always found a warm welcome at my aunt's house.

I remember meeting the Envoy Extraordinary of the Shah of Persia while on his way to Petrograd to present the Empress with a magnificent necklace of enormous pearls and the Tzarevitch with a portait of the Shah.

Two days after I met him again at a large

IN THE CAUCASUS

dinner-party at the Swetchines'—Mr Swetchine was governor of Tiflis.

·My Uncle de Nicolay had known this Persian official, with his strangely languorous brilliant eyes, when he was merely Persian Consul-General during my uncle's governorship, the cholera epidemic at that period having brought the two together in their work of mercy.

This parvenu — he was nothing more nor less—has since become Highness, Prince, Envoy and Ambassador-Extraordinary of the Shah, in spite of his humble past; enough success to bring hope to the most despairing heart.

During the envoy's youth he is reputed to have sold oranges; then he became a valet; and subsequently married an English governess at Tiflis whom he exchanged later on for a French girl.

Amongst the guests were several Turks and Persians wearing their fezes, which seemed absolutely a part of themselves. The effect was extremely picturesque. I must not forget the Emperor's envoy whom he had sent from Petrograd to greet this important personage.

Persia and Turkey went so far as to offer me mounts, but the idea of being accompanied by fezes made me reflect and decline the offer with many thanks.

Monsieur Swetchine was the nephew of the famous Madame Swetchine, well known for her writings and, also, for her conversion to the

Catholic Faith, her death being mourned by many friends in Paris.

A well-known big game hunter, Monsieur Swetchine often took part in the Grand Duke's boar hunts, hunts which would make our Western sportsmen's mouths water. Those boars are real giants; he had then killed forty without counting the pheasants, and jackals galore.

The French Consul, also, and his wife were most kind to me.

One day I was taken to St Mzchette, to which we drove in an old tumble-down vehicle drawn by four horses, returning by moonlight across those vast plains where cattle and sheep are bred and the cultivation of wine carried out more and more every year. We followed la Route Militaire—the Georgian Military Road—which winds across the mountains of Caucasia 132 miles away; at intervals we obtained lovely views over the plains and church of Didoubée, a place of pilgrimage, as we followed the course of the Koura.

The Georgian Military Road was made by order of the Empress Catherine; 800 soldiers were employed on the work, and in 1783 Count Paul Potiomkin—then in command of the Russian troops in the Caucasus—drove to Tiflis behind eight horses, the first man to make a carriage journey across the range. However, his first measure had been to build the fort of Vladikavkaz. Till then, nothing but a rough bridle-

SCENERY IN THE CAUCASUS

IN THE MOUNTAINS OF THE CAUCASUS

path was to be found, this in spite of the ancient race migrations from Asia into Europe and of the many military powers who had marched successively against the Caucasus: Egyptian, Scythian, Greek, Persian, Arab, Mongol, Tartar, Turk.

St Mzchette is the cradle as well as the burial place of the Kings of Georgia, and we visited the tombs of Prince Bagration-Moucransky and of Prince Grouzinsky of Georgia.

The cathedral is a fine building and contains splendid frescoes, alas, mostly smothered with plaster.

We were shown a pulpit carved out of a tree which is supposed to contain our Lord's tunic. The passion of our Lord and the deaths of several of the Apostles are represented by wooden sculptures dating from A.D. 329. The church encloses the ancient miniature cathedral which was the original edifice.

Many monks are buried there and the whole is surrounded by a high wall with towers.

The beautiful Queen Thamar, a celebrated Queen of Georgia, whose palace was within the precincts, could not have felt very happy there, one would imagine. But who can tell!

We lunched at a most filthy inn, and subsequently visited a convent, the tiny church of which contains the remains of the first King of Georgia and of his wife; it was built by St Nina who is so greatly venerated in the Caucasus. The tower of the church is very ancient and possesses many architectural qualities. We were shown the nuns' dormitory ; their beds consist of planks of wood merely covered with a carpet, each has a single pillow but no bolster. I did pity those poor things !

CHAPTER IX

TIFLIS is a town of 100,000 inhabitants, built, as it were, at the bottom of a basin, surrounded by high mountains which in former days were wooded, now, however, absolutely bare owing to a terrible conflagration some years ago.

The view of the snow-capped Mount Kasbeck is one of the most beautiful to be obtained in that superb range.

The streets of the town were paved with rough cobbles placed in upright position making it almost impossible for pedestrians, so much so that for their convenience little smooth crossings are made at intervals. The horses of the country are as sure-footed as mules, and they go at full tilt down the streets which to my unaccustomed mind seemed more like precipices than anything else. But I never once saw any of these animals stumble.

I could not help remarking the strange get-up of the police at night; "night watchmen" as they are called, posted at various street corners armed with huge clubs. I took them to be robbers before their calling was explained to me.

Apart from the European quarter of Tiflis there is also the Mussulman quarter, which is most interesting and its aspect most picturesque with its curious looking cosmopolitan populace.

It is wiser for a woman not to venture alone into this quarter, in spite of the amiable smiles and brilliant and inviting eyes of the Turks and Persians, who try to attract you into their pretty little shops so full of *cachet*. Many make carpets, some of which are very beautiful. The Persian bakers' shops are full of originality with their different loaves, not resembling ours in the least, and their large and flat pastry cakes which they hang on cords in their shop fronts, even several layers of these cakes one on the top of another where the glass front of the shops would be with us ; glass does not exist with them.

In the houses of the Caucasians there is always a vast divan covered with a sumptuous carpet ; which makes a very comfortable seat on which often five or six people crowd themselves, some sitting on the top after the manner of tailors. In the study or little drawing-room there are often besides great carpets hung on the wall which gives to the room a warm, furnished and comfortable look. The silver-work in the Caucasus is also very good, somewhat in the style of what you find in India. The country silks are of a beautiful colouring and are of a solidity beyond all question, even the taffeta, which is not the case with us.

This indeed is the East, the East beneath a sky perpetually blue and a climate which would make our Riviera green with envy.

Merchandise in this district was conveyed for the most part by camels and it was a common occurrence to see them in the streets of Tiflis.

TIFLIS—A PERSIAN BAKER'S SHOP

TIFLIS—A PERSIAN SHOEMAKER'S SHOP

IN THE CAUCASUS

From the windows of the train I was able to distinguish a caravan, numbering about eighty camels all in Indian file, silhouetted against the sky, on the edge of the Caspian, which the train skirts before it bends round the end of the mountains near Bakou and threads the valleys of Transcaucasia.

I have always admired those fine animals with their placid expression and their grand, slow, soft movements, which nothing seems to disturb.

The mineral wealth of the Caucasus is worthy of *The Arabian Nights*, but, unfortunately, owing to the non-existence of railways, it is next to impossible to utilize the output from but very few places.

The oil wells at Bakou and other places are, as every one knows, one of the great sources of the wealth of the country. Nothing is more terrible to behold than one of these oil-wells when it catches fire, which sometimes happens.

The Armenian church is interesting; the Armenians are known as the Jews of the Caucasus, and there is a saying that one Armenian is equal to five Jews!

There are two Catholic churches, one specially frequented by the Poles and built in the Polish quarter; the other built almost entirely by one of my grandmother's brothers, and where I used to go.

This grand-uncle of mine, Baron Louis de Nicolay, became a celebrated Russian General and conqueror of Shamyl, the famous Caucasian Chief held to be invincible till then in his mountains. This uncle ended his days as a monk at the Grande-Chartreuse, near Grenoble, in France, where he was known to the last, even by the visitors who always asked to see him, as " the old Russian General." He charmed them all in spite of himself by his brilliant intelligence and his charming gift of conversation; and they wondered how so much genius, hidden beneath the humble fustian of his frock, could adapt itself to the severe life of the cloister after the rough and free existence of a soldier and the emotions of the battle-field. The Superior allowed him a newspaper, a weak and solitary link to bind him to that world which had awarded him so many honours, but which he had left to be worthy of others more glorious.

A Protestant in his youth, he had been converted to the Catholic faith, during one of his visits to France, after several conversations with the well-known Monseigneur Dupanloup.

The monks of the Grande-Chartreuse made that delicious liqueur known everywhere under the name of Chartreuse—white and green. Certainly it is one of the best liqueurs procurable, and its good qualities are derived from the great purity of the ingredients used in its manufacture; the secret of its fine and strong flavour exists, they say, in certain plants and flowers collected by the monks in the mountains. The secret of its fabrication was only known to the Superior and in case of his death to one of the Fathers. Since the separation of Church and State in France the Carthusians have been expelled—an example

IN THE CAUCASUS

of the liberty of republics—and they have taken refuge in Spain, since when they have made a liqueur called Tarragone, which is not equal to the other, as, the flora not being the same, many of the first elements are missing.

Many princes of the country don the Caucasian costume, which is similar to the Cossack uniform; even the servants sometimes wear it and at first it was at times hard for me to make a distinction! One day I accompanied Lise Cheremetieff, Madame Arapoff, *née* Princesse Galitzine, and several other young women from the Dragoon and other regiments on a bicycle picnic in the neighbourhood of Tiflis; there were also present a few officers. We lunched gaily in the garden of a little country inn; and all went well till our return, but then our luck changed. Madame Arapoff fell and had the misfortune to sprain both her ankles. We had to hoist her into one of the carriages which followed. Three officers also found themselves unseated, and, as for me, I went over my handle bar, right in the middle of a descent, and picked myself up off a bed of pointed stones, which I found very hard in the Caucasus. I had as escort "Romeo"—an officer so nicknamed—who was also thrown off; he sang, danced and said a thousand foolish things. A little behind us followed a *moucha* or porter, a giant who carried my bicycle like a feather on one of his shoulders. We caught up the others at the tobacco manufactory. Then I got into the carriage with Madame Arapoff, when what was my astonishment to see her take from her muff two little slippers, most fascinating to behold, and put them on!

By what mystery were these two little slippers in her muff? That is a question that I have not yet solved—but, after all, a mystery is always insoluble or it ceases to be one any longer, and the mysterious has so much charm.

In these smart regiments one found the greatest diversity of types—a subject for interesting study—from the most refined from North Russia to that of the Tartar prince, very powerful but also very savage, I thought; the women were very elegant, many being dressed by Paquin.

We had the bad luck to miss at Tiflis Count Worontsoff-Dachkoff, the new governor of the Caucasus, and a friend of my aunt's, who was expected shortly.

There in the depth of the Caucasus one did not notice the war as in the north of Russia; indeed, one would hardly have realized it except for the departure of Prince Petia Troubetzkoy and a few others, and the visits we paid to Madame Cheremetieff—the Dowager—whom we always found surrounded by cases for the Red Cross, which she painted white herself, adding a big red Cross. She must certainly have flooded the Empire with them. She was very nice looking, and very amiable and distinguished.

At the end of December my aunt and I retraced our steps to Petrograd, in a direct route, having to renounce once again the Crimea and the Volga, as on our coming, my aunt's health not permitting the longer journey. I regretted it, for it would have been delightful and full of interest.

We bore the journey very well in spite of the three days and four nights in the train, during which time I found myself again much admiring three things : the banks of the Don, the country of the Cossacks ; the Caucasus range ; and the shores of the Caspian Sea, especially by moonlight.

The love of liberty, of war, of rapine are the chief characteristics of the Cossacks. They are excellent warriors and believe themselves superior to all other races. The power of Russia only makes itself felt in their country by troops which are quartered there. They look upon these soldiers as so many intruders, and despise the Russian peasant, whom they consider coarse and savage.

The Cossack does not work at home ; the young girl is allowed to do nothing, but may amuse herself to her heart's content ; a married woman must work very hard up to even the most advanced age. She must be submissive and laborious, like the woman of the East.

Apparently resigned, the Cossack woman has nevertheless in her home more real authority than the woman of the West.

The Cossack would not like to treat her familiarly in the presence of strangers, but *tête-à-tête* he acknowledges her supremacy and realizes that it is to her that he owes all that goes towards making the home comfortable. Thanks to this severe regime, the Cossack woman develops both morally and physically ; she possesses much good sense, and above all great firmness of character; she is very superior to the men of her race. Her beauty is a mixture of the women of northern Russia and the Tcherkesse or mountaineer type. She wears their costume: Tartar chemisette, with an embroidered jacket, Tartar shoes, and on the head the coloured handkerchief that the Russian peasant also wears. She is clean, and is careful about her dress.

The Cossack makes his own wine; and does not look upon drunkenness as a vice, but as a custom to which he should strictly conform.

A terrible snowdrift blocked our progress during several hours in the Russian Steppes. It seemed as though it would have been impossible to advance. In England we have no idea what these snowstorms are like.

At Rostoff on the Don, as on our outward journey, we walked a little way, taking this opportunity for a little air and exercise. At the station library awaiting a purchaser, I saw some French novels for sale, a choice which astonished me on account of their insignificance. I should never have expected to find them so far away. Possibly as a last resource!

On the other hand, at the Petrograd libraries one only sees the lightest French literature well exposed in the front row in the windows, those which we should refuse to read in France, the Russians pretending to believe that all French books are of that description. This made me furious; the falseness of the argument exasperated me, and I used to answer that they must evidently

IN THE CAUCASUS

have been chosen and written specially for the Russian market, for in France one never heard them spoken of.

Moscow, the real capital of Russia, which one feels so well to be the soul of this great people, and which had enchanted me in October during the too short hours which I spent there, enchanted me again with its Kremlin, its gilded cupolas, its Chinese town, its Red Square, old cannons. The old cannon balls heaped around, which had been taken from Napoleon, made my heart ache; but the city enchanted me more than ever, seen thus beneath its snow mantle.

May Russia become the tomb of the barbarous Hun—and may that day be not too long delayed. May the real Russia, the real great invincible Russia, though dumb at this moment, speak behind those high walls of the Kremlin, make herself heard, collect herself and understand her folly, and refuse to be any more the plaything and the prey of an enemy as detested as detestable, of an enemy who scoffs at her as it scoffed at her former sovereigns.

The sleeping-carriages in this Caucasus train were comfortable, but much in them was primitive. Thus each compartment was only lighted by one solitary smoky candle, of bad quality, which guttered very much, fixed in a sort of stand of the simplest kind, placed above the door leading to the corridor. When it went out, there was nothing to do but gaze on the darkness and call the attendant, who was often a long time in coming. The heating also was of the most primitive kind, consisting of a horrible little cheap stove placed at the end of every carriage, near the corridor by the exit, and all stuffed with birch wood. A pipe ran the length of the carriage, which was thus warmed.

When we arrived at Petrograd the thermometer was more than ten degrees Réaumur below zero; so cold was it that, when opening one's mouth to speak, it seemed as though one had been stabbed to the heels by cold steel.

The cold is doubly increased by the wind—and at Petrograd it nearly always blows hard—tearing with violence along the canals which traverse the town in all directions.

As at Tiflis many friends and relations had come to the station with flowers and bonbons; it is a charming custom, I think. Among them was Uncle Cherwachidze, who in spite of his wish to join us in the Caucasus, which he adores, had been unable to do so on account of his important duties at the Court. Some years before, the younger brother of the Emperor, Grand Duke George, had come to the Caucasus on account of his health, being consumptive, and one day, on his return from a motor drive with my uncle, he died in the latter's arms. It is since that time that the Empress-Dowager has shown my uncle so great an attachment and friendship that she cannot bear to be separated from him for long.

I brought back from the Caucasus a memory that was sunny and full of gratitude for the charming welcome that I found there. My aunt often gives me news from there and old friends still send me their remembrances, and with all my heart I send them the same.

The Caucasian has the right to be proud of his beautiful country, with its ever blue sky and its ever temperate climate which seems to give him that wonderful *joie-de-vivre* expression which appeals so deeply to the stranger, who is always struck by that warm and unforgettable charm of welcome which greets him at every turn.

Part III
AT PETROGRAD

CHAPTER X

ON the 6th January 1905—Old Style—
I made my entry into the most brilliant
and exclusive society of Petrograd, and
the occasion was for the annual blessing
of the Neva on the feast of the Epiphany.

I was invited to witness the ceremony at the Winter Palace in the quality of " distinguished foreigner."

A small pavilion shaped like an ancient circular Greek temple, with pillars, open on all sides, had been erected on the frozen waters of the river in front of the Palace. In the centre a hole was pierced in the ice, until the waters were reached, when a bucket was lowered and brought up brimfull; this water was then blessed by the Archimandrite, some set aside for the blessing of newborn babes, and some for subsequently blessing all the colours of the various regiments quartered at Petrograd; the rest of the water was poured back into the hole in the ice, and thenceforth mingled with the river and then the whole Neva was blessed!

Formerly it was considered of the utmost importance that new-born infants should be completely immersed in the Neva—immersed as the rite of the Greek Church demands. It has been asserted on the best authority that the Archbishop, when his hands were petrified with cold, would sometimes let a child slip in, merely remarking indifferently, " Give me another."

I drove up to the Palace in my Uncle de Baranoff's Court equipage—I was staying with them at the time—which was drawn by a pair of prancing black horses, the men wearing scarlet and gold liveries contrasting vividly with the dazzling whiteness of the snow.

I was met at the foot of the staircase and escorted by Vicomte de Salignac-Fénelon, an attaché at the French Embassy, who whispered in my ear very discreetly :

" We may shortly be reduced to ashes."

" If that is so," said I, " we shall die in good company."

Every one at that time felt that he was living on a volcano, the formidable irruption of which might break out at any moment.

The various members of the Diplomatic Corps asked to be presented to me in turn, amongst them Count Berchthold, at that time Councillor at the Austro-Hungarian Embassy, who, since then and up to the time the war broke out, has played such an important rôle in his country's affairs, subsequently becoming Austrian Ambassador in Petrograd before the war and then Minister for Foreign Affairs in Vienna at the beginning of the war.

It is a privilege granted to Hungarian diplomats to wear their Magyar costumes on all State occasions, and certainly Count Berchthold was strikingly distinguished looking in his !

On the arm of the Dutch Minister, Monsieur de Wedde, I reached the Grand Ball-room and passed between the brilliant escort of Chevaliers-Gardes and Gardes-à-Cheval, besides others decked out in their magnificent uniforms, forming a cordon round each room.

At last we reached the room reserved for the *corps diplomatique*, where every one was assembled in front of the windows overlooking the Chapel erected on the Neva.

The clergy were wearing their most superb sacerdotal robes and ornaments, escorting the Emperor, the Grand Dukes and all the Court in procession. The spectacle was most imposing, rendered all the more so by the white mantle which was over all !

Presently there entered the drawing-room in which we were assembled the two Empresses and Grand Duchesses Xenia, Olga—both sisters of the Emperor—Marie Pavlovna and others dressed in their elaborate Russian Court costumes. This consists of velvet robes with round deep *décolletage* and long trains, and wearing on their heads the *kakochnik* scintillating with pearls, diamonds and other precious stones.

Some were in blue, others in pale green, bright pink, red, etc.; the ladies-in-waiting and maids-of-honour dress in the colour of the Grand Duchess, to whose court they belong.

Their trains were borne by pages from the well-known *corps des pages*.

I noticed again my Uncle Cherwachidze wearing his grand uniform, covered with gold lace and orders of every description—he seemed more than ever to form part of the train of his Empress.

Then came the Court and the clergy, defiling into the room next to ours, the latter intoning some wonderful Russian chants, which are so perfectly rendered that one imagines them to be instrumentally accompanied.

The anticipated attempt at assassination was not long delayed : presently some fragments of shrapnel shells fell into our room and quite close to the group of people where I was standing, smashing the panes of glass of one of the windows, which were strewn all over the floor. These shells had been fired from the Fortress of St Peter and St Paul situated on the opposite side of the Neva.

Ostensibly the guns were fired as a salute with blank cartridges, but through an oversight of the commanding officer one had been fired with live shells, the result being that a perfect hail of shrapnel fell on to the Chapel in which the Emperor had taken up his position, he of course being the object aimed at.

The Tzar during this terrible ordeal never moved a muscle except to make the Sign of the Cross.

I shall never forget the quiet resigned smile on His Imperial Majesty's countenance when he returned to the Palace—it seemed almost unearthly. In the street an unfortunate mounted policeman was killed, and on the floor beneath ours—the ground floor—five people were seriously wounded.

Seeing that the Emperor was safe we congratulated ourselves by saying: " Comme c'est chic! Nous avons eu même un attentat! "

After having met a number of friends, ladies and gentlemen in waiting, I was conducted into the dining-room on the arm of Monsieur Merghelynck, Councillor of the Belgian Legation, where a copious luncheon at small tables was prepared, and which we partook of with relish in spite of the regrettable incident.

Each table was presided over by a maid-of-honour, ours being a very cosmopolitan one, made up principally of diplomats, Russians, Germans, Austrians, and even a Turk.

On my right sat the War Minister, Sakharoff, who not long afterwards fell a victim to a bomb outrage.

Fate seemed to decree that poor Merghelynck should be continually the victim of some tragedy or other: he was in China during the siege of Pekin by the Boxers, where for his gallant behaviour while helping to defend the French legation he was the proud recipient of the Legion of Honour; he was in Serbia when King Alexander and Queen Draga were assassinated; and now that he is dead even his ashes are not allowed to remain in peace, for he was buried at or near Ypres, which is now, alas, only a heap of ruins.

During the winter 1904-1905 no ball took place at the Palace, both on account of the war with Japan and also on account of the internal troubles, so unfortunately I am unable to give a description of the supper which under ordinary conditions would have taken place in the Great Palm Hall which I had hoped to admire so much.

At Petrograd one is continually coming across small chapels at unexpected places, erected on the site of some Nihilist outrage against members of the Imperial family.

The Russian makes a great show of his religion, and he places an Icon in every room of his house, hung in a corner, very high up, just under the ceiling; and he causes every room in his house to be blessed once a year.

At my Aunt de Baranoff's the annual ceremony is carried out to the letter. Each member of the family, holding in his right hand a candle, follows in procession the " Winter Palace " pope, with his long curly hair carefully arranged, while he carries out the blessing by sprinkling holy water on his way.

Three days after—Sunday, January 9th, 1905, henceforth to be remembered as " Le Dimanche Rouge "—occurred the first sign of the coming irruption which had been anticipated for so long.

For a whole week previously the police had posted hand-bills imploring the public not to venture out of doors that day as trouble was expected, and that the police could not be held responsible for what might happen.

The day dawned more gloomily than usual, it had snowed hard all the previous night and it was still snowing. I witnessed the extraordinary and terrible sight of the crowd of malcontents and revolutionaries from the windows of 6 Millionne, where I was staying with my uncle, General de Baranoff. The Winter Palace was situated on the large square at the end of our street, quite near, so I could not be better placed. It was on the direct route to it. They kept on passing in small groups from early dawn, until they had become one compact mass beneath the windows of the Winter Palace, for Gapon, their leader, had ordered them to assemble at 2 p.m. in the huge palace square.

These misguided creatures were carrying all manner of implements, some even shouldered scythes, in fact anything they could get hold of, I expect. All wore a sad look of arrogance and disorder, even the children. Many of the women carried heavy bundles as if they intended to leave their homes for ever.

The doors and gates of every house and courtyard had been closed with heavy chains for fear of invasion and pillage. One felt more than ever that one was living on a volcano—and a very live one too—belching forth the most formidable elements of destruction.

Several times the Chevaliers-Gardes charged amongst the crowd; at first slowly but effectively—under our windows—until the mob was hurled back.

My poor aunt was terribly frightened, and forbade me to go out that day, consequently I did not witness any of the bloody scenes which occurred, but which the papers grossly exaggerated. The Emperor and Empress showed themselves to the crowd from one of the bal-

H

conies of the Palace, and their appearance seemed to have rather a soothing effect.

Many blamed the Emperor, others the army for the sanguinary rôle that was played that day, but what else could they have done under the circumstances?

The police organization was nil: Trepoff, its future head, had not as yet come to the fore. Three times the mob was summoned to disperse, three times they were warned what would be the result of their refusing to do so; but their only answer was sullen inertia and threatening.

Had not vigorous measures been taken at once, it is my firm belief that the Emperor would have shared the fate of Louis XVI.

Firing went on in the Nevsky Prospect and the Morskaia. We heard shots whistling past continually.

The Chevaliers-Gardes were obliged to make several simultaneous charges along the quays and other places that night.

The mob was not armed and remained silent. Their action was decidedly revolutionary, but it was by no means a general rising of a whole people in revolt. It was to be regretted that many quite innocent people who showed themselves in the streets out of curiosity were to be counted amongst the dead and wounded—but that was, of course, their own look out, as they should have hearkened to the warning.

Equipages were overturned; the malcontents stripped a general of all his clothes in spite of the cold, and then beat him. A young officer was thrown into a canal; and we were warned by a friend on the telephone from the Winter Palace that it was dangerous even to set foot in the street.

My poor Aunt de Baranoff was more terrified than ever, and told me in a trembling voice: "On no account turn on the electric light for fear of the revolutionaries firing into the windows"—in Russia there are no shutters—"and entering the house and murdering us all." This in spite of the fact of our house being part of the Palace of the Grand Duke, then Crown Property, and our courtyard filled with soldiers; so we consequently lived several days by candlelight, which seemed rather gloomy after the gorgeous light of the many chandeliers.

Gapon and several other leaders had really deceived these credulous masses and led them to believe that they would, by demonstrating, induce the Tzar to accede to their demands; but it was not long before the masses found out that they were being made the tools of their leaders' own ambitions to bring about a great political manifestation. Thus, discontent and loss of faith soon spread amongst them.

The most sinister news appeared in the papers on the following day, stating that the populace would be now supplied with bombs and firearms, that houses would be broken into and pillaged, but there proved to be no foundation for these anticipated fears.

However, there was still some disturbance

that night, and fighting took place in the Sadovaia; but there was no bloodshed.

I dined that evening at the French Embassy and, as I drove through the streets, Petrograd seemed to be a changed city: troops bivouacking everywhere, rifles piled together, the soldiers and horses keeping warm beside huge beacon fires, the flames from which cast a lurid light over all the vast stretch of frozen snow.

The only Russians at dinner were Prince Dolgorouky and Baron de Ramsay—whose wife is English—the others having at the eleventh hour sent excuses: they had all contracted chills!

I had been obliged to keep my horses standing from an early hour, for the police order had gone forth that no carriage was to leave the stable after 7 p.m., as they feared trouble and as equipages were looked upon askance.

In case of the revolutionaries carrying out their threat of cutting the electric wires, the French Ambassadress drew our attention to a system by which all the candles in the dining-room could be lighted instantaneously by means of a connecting resinous tape, thus replacing the electricity.

The idea of placing the city under martial law was seriously entertained. The Palace and town were guarded by the military for many days; after that patrols went through the streets on business bent.

Every anniversary celebration in its turn made people dread a fresh outburst of disorder.

AT PETROGRAD

The failure to arrest Gapon surprised me very much. It was said in Petrograd that the authorities dare not make use of their powers. He played the most ignoble rôle and worked on the superstitious masses by dressing himself up in his sacerdotal robes—he was a pope—and with his hands aloft holding a crucifix he urged them on; then, again, he would make use of all kinds of disguises and appeared to be everywhere at the same time.

For a long time past he had rented a house in Petrograd, where he gave lectures, befriended by the Empress-Dowager and Grand Duchess Xenia. He was well informed about every detail concerning the secret police.

The money for this revolution—of which he was the life and soul—came from abroad, as is always the case where revolutions are concerned; the revolutionaries themselves were given three times the amount of their ordinary pay. Amongst the dead and wounded were many students disguised as women.

The most terrifying reports were circulated all over the town: Petrograd was to be set on fire, the nobles were to be massacred, while their properties were to be burnt and pillaged; this had already occurred in many places, notably in the Baltic provinces, of which the population consists of German-speaking people and is for the most part Lutheran.

Gapon and the other leaders preached to the peasants that the ground they cultivated was their own, their very own; that the nobles and the wealthy classes were robbing them, attributing to themselves certain rights which they had no business to possess—all the tenets which Lenin has preached to-day.

Tempers ran high in those days. Several stores of arms were pillaged and their contents stolen.

After his flight from Russia, Gapon, from his German lair, continued to issue pamphlets in the hope of creating more disturbance in the minds of his followers. A few months later he was most unexpectedly found dead, hanging from a beam in an uninhabited *datcha* or villa at Ozerky, on the line to Finland, near Petrograd.

As one can readily understand, the results achieved were not the fruits of the effort of a day, but rather of an organized labour, planned with the greatest care and followed with the greatest perseverance, accompanied by all the treachery and all the brutality of the Hun.

CHAPTER XI

I MET in society many who were much imbued with the idea of a constitution, and even of a Republic, a word which sounded like magic to them—magic, like something far off. They reminded me both by their advanced ideas and by their occasional indifference of the spirit about which I had often read : of the spirit that must have reigned at the Court of France on the eve of the Great Revolution. The Russian Empire, composed as it is of a number of races so diversely opposed to one another—neither sharing the same sentiments nor possessing any interest in common, races between which even a certain animosity exists always, an enormous population of uneducated, half savage people—would render, it seems to me, a Republic out of the question. I wrote of this twelve years ago !

Many an illusion has already taken wings at the sight of what is passing now, and of that which is bound to come. In the future we may not see the Great Republic dreamt of by Kerensky and others, but rather the destruction of Great Russia itself, and a collection of little republics springing up, small not by the narrowness of the confines of such, but by the weakness of their constitutions, which shall be either completely independent one from the other, or else bound together by the most slackened Federal system. They will probably be penetrated and dominated by German influence.

Where will be the dreams of those who thought to perceive in a republic a special autonomy for their province and with it complete liberty? It is necessary for this great homogeneous nation to be ruled by one hand, and it is essential that that hand should be a firm one.

Kerensky himself admitted that when he was in power. But why it must be so plebeian a hand is what I cannot understand. Kerensky has tried and has promptly proved himself to be a complete failure. He was bound to fail, all goes from bad to worse, and one must completely cease to count on the military or the political support of that Power, even up to quite recently so great; and thus it will be till the end of the war and for long after.

The absolutely powerless government of Kerensky dared not undertake anything against the agitators Lenin and Co., for it knew well that it had no real force behind it. It is this weakness, both voluntary and compulsory, that ruined it, and it has after a short period been overthrown by those terrible Extremists, with Lenin, that chattel of Germany, at their head, for he has been bought with their gold. As one of my uncles wrote to me some time ago: "If Germany raises a statue to Hindenburg she should also raise one to Lenin and to

AT PETROGRAD

his Bolshevik companions. It is their doctrine more than anything else that has caused the demoralization of our army and the successes of our enemies.

"The Bolsheviks are the Communards of France of 1871 who are left unrestrained for the sake of sane principle until it is perceived too late that to allow these mad fanatics to speechify and act leads to ruin."

No really Russian soldier has fired a shot since the Revolution except against his own officers —a great number of whom have fallen—or against his own Allies when these would not pack off before the Boches without striking a blow. The victories of July 1917, such as they were, were brought off by Finns, Letts, Lithuanians, and Poles, with Czech-Slovak prisoners who had been set at liberty. All these were not fighting for Russia, but for their own liberty and autonomy, which depended on a German defeat.

One can only affirm one thing to-day, and that is that without the Revolution the situation would have been even worse than at present, for a separate peace would long ago have been concluded, thanks to the intrigues of the ex-Empress, perjured to all which should have been most dear to her, and of the traitors who surrounded her and conspired with her to baffle, blind, drug and intimidate that unlucky and ill-fated puppet, the ex-Emperor, a man with no will, no force of character; honest in himself but incapable of exacting honesty from those around him, and always agreeing with the last person who had spoken to him.

Her moujiks are the latent force of Russia, not the agitators of her towns and capitals, and they will be the first to see the falseness of the doctrines of the spies with which they are fed to gain this concurrence. May the moujik not recognize too late that he is being lured away —and who lures him? The ignoble Russian Bolo, his pockets filled with German gold, recompense of his treachery. That is the whole story.

The task of the Russian Bolo would not have been as simple if a Tzar worthy of the moment were still there. The moujik no longer has his " Little Father," of whom he made almost a god. For him he would have died with joy, with all that fanaticism which can possess the Russian soul, that fanaticism would have made of him an invincible soldier—but why should he die for a Kerensky? He is not a " Little Father," he is a man like himself—and at that he demurs. Can one blame these hardy and simple workers of the great steppes if they find themselves adrift, no longer having either him to adore who was almost their god on earth, or that to venerate which was the religion of their *izba* [1] for centuries? For the Tzar was not only the head of the State, but also the head of the Religion of his State, the Greek Orthodox Church, as it is called over there. " He is our pope," Russians often said to me, referring to my Roman Pope.

[1] Izba is the Russian word for peasant hut.

For who was Kerensky ? Kerensky is of the people and a barrister. His father was or is still the master of a small school. A student at the time of the first Revolution in 1905, he was arrested as a Socialist and Revolutionary. No one spoke of him then, he was quite unknown, and he was arrested like many others; but the circumstance has been recalled to-day.

He has often been called " Russia's strong man "; after the deposition of the Tzar he seized the power. He was a Social Democrat, or Minimalist. His empire over the masses was enormous; but it began to diminish when he developed in statesmanship. The Extremists were not slow to see this, and acted on it. The Soviet, which was supposed to support his Provisional Government, was only composed of so-called Russians, who were simply all Germans and for the most part Jews.

Lenin himself, the chief of the Extremists, Maximalists, is a notorious Hun agent, and is known throughout Europe as a dangerous leader. For some years his activities, though confined to Russia, have been exercised on behalf of Germany. His doctrine may be summed up thus :

1. The immediate conclusion of the war.
2. The handing over of the land to the peasants.
3. The settlement of the economic crisis.

Trotsky is an Extreme Anarchist, well known to the police in most European countries. Before the declaration of war he was at New York, where he spent some months. On his way to Russia, in March 1917, he was detained at Halifax by the English Authorities, who released him on an appeal which came to them from the Russian Government.

The Soviet is the Council of Workmen's and Soldiers' Delegates ; it is to their influence that must be ascribed much of the present chaotic condition of the country.

One of the great faults of the Government which has succeeded the Empire has been to allow the return of all these dangerous agitators who had taken refuge beyond the frontier of the great empire and who were only worthy of Siberia. Korniloff was the well-known chief of the Cossacks and also the ex-commander and chief of the Armies. He, with true insight, saw the danger his country was running; seeing her drifting to anarchy he did all he could to make Kerensky act firmly. The latter refusing to do so, he took the affairs into his own hands, but failed, and was to have been tried for revolt. Had Korniloff been lucky he might have saved his country.

There remains yet one hope in the powerful chief of the Don Cossacks, Kaledin, under whose orders is the south of Russia. May he succeed in restoring a firm Monarchy.

The reform of certain matters necessary to our century ought to have started from above.

It is certain that if the Emperor had wished

to listen to the advice that sensible people had given him, instead of listening to his wife and the little clique of ignorant and blind reactionaries which surrounded her—and from the heart of which she insisted on recruiting the ministers, etc.—the goal would have been reached.

It was in vain that Grand Duke Nicholas wrote to the Emperor denouncing the plot that was forming against him and so near him; it was in vain that several times he came to see the Tzar trying to convince him; but it was all to no avail.

The task of reform would not have been easy for anyone; and was quite beyond the powers of Nicholas II. The fault was partly due, it is said, to the fact that the early education of the Emperor was never that of a child who had, in perspective, the heavy task of governing a great empire, but mainly in the man himself.

Russia needed an intelligent, energetic ruler, full of action and decision, and not this victim of an invincible obstinacy, often a symptom of crass stupidity. It would have been necessary that he should have had enough force and courage to have dismissed the insolent, the incapable, the Germans at heart if not in race who surrounded and dominated him.

But let us return to 1905. The partisans of the aristocracy greatly deplored the fact of Prince Troubetzkoy and his followers being received by the Emperor.

The Protestants, and even some Russians with advanced notions, held this to be sublime, a great step towards liberty and deliverance. The part played by Troubetzkoy and his friends resembled that of those nobles who, at the beginning of the Great French Revolution, abandoned their king and themselves became the first victims of the infuriated mob. The mere fact of their having been received by the Emperor was sufficient to cause the latter a great loss of prestige in the eyes of the masses. Nothing could have had a more disastrous effect on them, and to think of those malcontents being well received—the last people who should have been.

"Ils auront été se faire photographier," exclaimed one of my uncles, " mais ils n'obtiendront rien de ce qu'ils désirent."

The truth of this assertion was to be felt the next day when all the papers were full of the account, with illustrations of the reception.

The Revolutionary party was formidably and admirably organized; one felt that this revolution which was commencing was the outcome of long premeditated plans: its fibres had penetrated everywhere, even where one least expected to find them, and one can hardly imagine the perfect accord, the power, and the methods employed by these disorganizers of public order, moral tranquillity and love of country. Every day in Petrograd alone there were a number of political arrests, plots unveiled, bombs discovered.

Those miserable Nihilists were prepared to die without a murmur, as if really inspired, like regular fanatics, when obliged to give their lives, never consenting to divulge anything to the police, not even to give their names, and that in spite of the most cruel tortures used to make them speak; and they often believed themselves to be martyrs to a good and sacred cause.

The names of young men and girls of the best society, whose fathers more often than not held important positions, were mentioned as being connected with them.

There was much talk then of an arrest which had taken place in the heart of the society to which a certain young girl belonged. She had hired a little flat in Petrograd, where she had many relations and friends as well known from their social position as from the important appointments they held.

Who could have ever believed that she could have affiliated herself with these sectaries and been a party to their conspiracy. Precisely for this reason she was chosen by the revolutionaries who deposited in her care their papers and documents, believing them to be thus in safety.

This girl had been in Switzerland the year before, and had there made the acquaintance of a young man who was actually one of the most active chiefs of the Nihilist party. This man designedly paid attention to her, and she became madly in love with him. They met again during the winter in Petrograd, and resolved to assassinate Trepoff—the chief of police. In order to achieve this they decided to station at the great Morskaia, nearly opposite his house, a man dressed as a commissionaire. Here I may explain that, in Petrograd, there were at many of the cross streets depots of commissionaires wearing red caps; they carried letters, etc., for the smallest emolument. But this man was badly chosen; being a very good-looking youth he attracted the notice of the others, the real commissionaires, who warned the police. These latter observed him, arrested him, and found that he carried a bomb.

Of the large band who had plotted the assassination, the majority were arrested.

Our young heroine was arrested at her hairdresser's just as she was going to the Opera. Her father, governor of a province, was anything but pleased to learn of the conduct of his daughter, of whose advanced ideas he had no suspicion.

A few days later two sisters, well-known also in Petrograd society, attempted suicide. These were the Princess X . . . and Mademoiselle Trepoff, friends of the aforementioned. The Princess shot herself with a revolver and her life was in danger for many days, but she recovered at the end of that time. It was the same with her sister, who threw herself under a train at the Nicholas station. I had met her only a few days before. It is said that since then she has to wear a heel made of metal to replace the one reduced to a pulp by the wheels of the train. When recovered they reappeared in society without exhibiting any shame. Incredible, is it not?

Some spoke of an unhappy love affair, others of politics; my humble opinion is the general one, that they found themselves compromised by the arrest of their friend.

The affair was suppressed, thanks to the influence of their Uncle Trepoff, the chief of police, and without any ill-feeling, poor man, on his part!

Every day some fresh bomb explosion took place, causing many victims in some part or other of the Empire.

One day I happened to be walking on the Champs de Mars — where so many of the Revolutionaries who perished last March [1917] now lie buried in their red coffins—when my attention was drawn to a certain individual with a most evil countenance walking a few paces in front of me; when all of a sudden an *izvo* —diminutive of the word meaning " hackney carriage "—drew up quite close to me, and two men jumped out precipitately, throwing themselves on this individual and dragging him along with them into the carriage. One of them was a member of the military police, and the other a member of the secret police in plain clothes.

They had the greatest trouble to secure their prisoner, who was a most vigorous ruffian and made use of all his strength to free his hands so as to reach his coat pocket, which contained a bomb no doubt, and which he evidently intended to throw at one of the Grand Dukes, who happened to drive past in his equipage a few minutes later, while the cab with its struggling trio dashed off in another direction.

I wrote to one of my friends twelve years ago : " May Society here [Petrograd], so brilliant but often so light and so indifferent, not experience one day the horrors and crimes of our revolution in France of 1793."

People spoke, it is true, of the great and bloody contest that was unfolding itself in Manchuria with airs of deep regret, due, however, much more to the shame inflicted by successive defeats and by their notable inferiority than to the poignant feeling they should have experienced at seeing their country tried and unhappy. I thought them really much too philosophical ; it seemed to me as though they were talking about a war which did concern their country—Allied, perhaps, but not their own. The French war in the Soudan, though on so small a scale, made much more sensation in France. And yet how many homes were in mourning in Petrograd, in that society which I frequented, and of which alone I was in a position to judge.

The *salons* were partly closed and there were no balls, but the theatres were by no means empty, and on the evenings of the greatest reverses were full of uniforms of every branch of the forces; even on the evening when the great naval defeat of Tsussima—May the 14th, the anniversary of Coronation Day—which scattered and destroyed the fleet, was known at Petrograd, the Russian Opera and the theatres were crowded with naval officers. This disaster did not occur as a surprise to poor Admiral Rogestvensko, for he had felt he was going to his doom. For the rest, this regrettable aberration was remarked in high places, for the " Autocrat " made known by all the newspapers that these officers should not show themselves in public for some days at least.

On the 17th of February Grand Duke Sergius-Alexandrovitch, Governor-General of Moscow, was blown to atoms in the streets of Moscow, an event which came as a real shock to me. I remember my Uncle de Baranoff being at once informed by telephone of his death.

It was said at the time that the Grand Duchess had run to the place of assassination and, flinging herself on the remains of her dead husband, had recovered his brains and wrapped them in her handkerchief.

The Grand Duke was not a good husband, and beautiful as she was—an elder sister of the Empress—their home was not a happy one.

Ever since her husband's death she has devoted her life to acts of charity.

All attempts against Trepoff, chief of the police, failed that year, he having to resort to every kind of ruse to escape, even going so far as to drive about concealed in a post and telegraph van.

Bombs were to be expected in a crowd; in churches; in fact, everywhere!

CHAPTER XII

THE Court left Petrograd for Tsarskoe-Celo in January 1905, not to return again for two years.

The Empress lived in constant dread of some misfortune befalling the Emperor or the Tzarevitch, and had to endure the most cruel tortures in consequence. Not a day passed without there being some plot discovered, and once, even, an infernal machine was found connected by wires to the infant's bed when he was but a few months old!

The Empress, tall and still a beautiful woman, had, however, no longer the delicate beauty which I believe she possessed at the time of her marriage. She was very cold in appearance and manner—perhaps due to shyness as some affirm—and in conversation never seemed to have the courage to start a subject, possibly finding nothing to say.

The notion that this limitation is necessary to a Sovereign-Lady is negatived by the conversational powers of the Queen of Italy, for instance, who expatiates upon the doings of the King, of herself and her children from the time of their rising—very early, as I was informed by Her Majesty, and from which I decided that it is not worth while to be a

Queen—till they go to bed : a flowing stream of information.

In spite of all this sad state of affairs the winter passed for me like a dream.

My friends Monsieur et Madame de Saint-Pair, a charming distinguished couple, were kindness itself to me, and it was not long before I got to know all the *corps diplomatique.* I was invited on their reception days and to their parties, and of course those of a great number of Russians.

On Mondays I dined and spent the evening at the French Embassy. Tuesdays the German Embassy received in the evenings. Thursdays it was Belgium's turn, and so on ; added to which there were afternoon receptions and luncheons and dinners—not a single day passed without my being engaged from morning till morning again.

I got dreadfully spoilt.

I was often taken to the Russian Opera at the Théâtre Marie ; the performance was very good, and Madame Litvinne one of the great attractions. Even in those days she was very stout, but less vast than when last I saw her in Paris. The lady seemed to realize that she displayed herself to better advantage by maintaining a front towards the audience than by exhibiting herself in profile.

She had married a Polish Count.

Those who respected themselves, and there were many whose desire it was to do so, had their stall at the ballet.

The Russian ballet, which had become so popular a feature of the last few pre-war Covent Garden seasons, has always been one of the most fashionable meeting-places of Petrograd society. I often went to the ballet and thoroughly enjoyed those evenings, being extremely amused always in contemplating the varied expressions on the physiognomies of both my young and old bachelor friends, with their eyes lost in rapt admiration—absolutely embedded in their opera-glasses. Certainly, the dancing was marvellous and the luxurious setting beyond description, exhibiting the most perfect and artistic taste imaginable.

The school of the ballet was an Imperial institution, entirely financed by the Crown. The stars were in receipt of enormous salaries, and those who were destined to make their career in the ballet started to learn their steps at the early age of three years.

All the very smartest and best-known people in society made a point of going to the ballet once or twice a week. Afterwards we went to supper at a restaurant—my weakness was for " l'Ours," then very much the fashion. The Théâtre Michel, where French plays were given, was also a great rendezvous, and during the intervals our box was always packed with visitors.

In summer, after an evening party or the theatre, we sometimes drove to the Islands—the Hyde Park of Petrograd. It was a delightful thing to do by the light of those white nights, and it filled one with joy. The streets and the bridges were sometimes so animated that the night seemed like day.

La Baletta—a pretty actress and a Jewess—was then in great favour and had attracted the attention of the Grand Duke Alexis.

Tongues were soon busy with this affair, and the Grand Duke was accused of having spent on her the funds intended for the fleet to buy her splendid jewels. To contradict this report she appeared on the stage without a single jewel.

The Grand Duke Alexis Alexandrovitch, brother of the late Emperor Alexander III., and son of Alexander II., the Tzar Liberator, had never ceased to mourn the death of his morganatic wife to whom he had been deeply attached. So greatly did he feel his loss that he was gradually pining away, and this sad state perturbed the whole of the Imperial family, who were in despair concerning the fate of poor Alexis, until one of their members, seeing La Baletta acting at the theatre, and being struck by her resemblance to the late " Grand Duchess," had the brilliant inspiration of bringing about a meeting between the disconsolate Grand Duke and the actress, with the result that " Xesis " fell head over ears in love with the lady, and immediately forgot all about his late wife.

They lived together for many years in Paris, after the disgrace into which the Grand Duke had fallen following on his scandalous sequestration of funds intended for naval purposes during his tenure of the post of Grand Admiral of the Fleet when the war with Japan was on, spending their winters in Pau and Biarritz, where they were always to be seen at the gambling tables of the Casino.

The Grand Duke died in exile in Paris about nine years ago, remaining faithful to La Baletta to the end; but rumour has it that she was left no money and, consequently, she was obliged to sell one by one her many beautiful jewels, until she was reduced to penury, dying a few years ago neglected and forgotten.

Many amusing tales were told about this couple and the people they met, but one of the drollest was that of a very vulgar rich American woman, who spent her time running after royalties during the latter's *villeggiatúra* at Biarritz, where she entertained them lavishly.

Mrs X . . . had often met the Grand Duke Alexis at the tables, but not being satisfied merely with a bowing acquaintance, one day approached H.I.H. and in a most drawling voice said: "Monseigneur, je vous prie de me présenter à Madame la grande-duchesse." To this remark Alexis at first paid no attention, but, on the request being repeated, he acceded to her wish; and she, all smiles and bows before La Baletta, drawled out again, "Très honorée, madame la grande-duchesse."

On another occasion my husband was standing

beside the Grand Duke and his companion at the tables when he overheard the Grand Duke remonstrate with La Baletta for not staking a certain winning horse, to which she replied: " Je l'aurais bien fait, monseigneur, si je possédais les coffres-forts de Votre Altesse."

Before the season for the Isles commenced, the quays at Petrograd were the favourite rendezvous, where one was sure to meet a number of friends, carriages being occupied for the most part by ladies wearing magnificent furs.

A party of about twenty of us used to meet every morning out skating—a very cosmopolitan lot composed of diplomats from all over Europe.

The daughters of Monsieur Mouravieff, then Minister for Foreign Affairs, and afterwards Russian Ambassador in Rome, where he died, used to join our party every day; Countess Berchthold came very often; also Mrs Napier, with her husband Colonel Napier, then Military Attaché to the British Embassy; and many others.

The skating rinks in Russia are very safe, as notwithstanding the great thickness of the ice they submerge large flat boats placed side by side up to a few inches below the water before it has frozen, so that if the ice breaks there is no danger of disappearing under the floes.

Nothing was more amusing once one had on one's skates than to let oneself be pushed by the wind, at a pace which sometimes reached a giddy speed.

My trembling steps made their debut between "Belgium" and "Holland," whose patience I admired, while little wooden seats—very heavy, too heavy to be upset—gave a precious help to the beginner.

Ski-ing was also much in favour, and one of my friends used to ski from Petrograd to Cronstadt in two hours. It must have been delightful to carve out a road for oneself through that immense, glittering whiteness; an excursion full of poetry and dreams, it seemed to me, in all the sadness of Nature at this season, which sleeps for many months under its thick white shroud—sleeps "as in a death."

The *troika* charmed me, especially for making long excursions, enveloped in warm furs, to the sound of pretty bells; one felt quite Russified. On one's veil the breath froze in the icy air and formed real stalactites.

The Russians recommend veils of white wool, made like light shawls, for this sort of expedition. I thought them dreadful, so unbecoming, a quite barbarous invention, but the only efficacious one against the cold.

As for the *Montagnes-russes*, or toboggan runs, and really "ice mountains" in Russian practice, nothing could be more heating, the descent being more than swift, so swift and so narrow that on each side there are planks forming walls to prevent a serious fall; but the emotion warms one up, and that is exactly what one needs in that country of ice and snow. This *Montagnes-russe* Club was charming and is situated on the island of Christophky, on the Islands.

These " mountains " consist, in fact, of a very high block of ice, as high as a house. One gains the summit by climbing a staircase of wood, which is behind. Arrived at the top, the cavalier places himself flat on his chest on a little flat steel sleigh; this steel is so slippery on the ice, and the beginning of the descent so near and so sudden, that it seems as if one would disappear into the abyss before the appointed time.

At the start of the sleigh the cavalier's head is over the abyss, and therefore much lower than his feet, and he guides the sleigh with his arms, which he stretches more or less on one side or another as he feels it necessary. I mounted behind him on another little sleigh of the same kind, but I knelt on it and sat on my heels, and there was only just room, the sleigh being very narrow; then I had to seize my cavalier's two legs, placing his two feet, shod with thick boots, one under each of my arms, holding tight and not letting go whatever happened. These two legs were one's only chance of ensuring a safe descent.

Once I felt my sleigh leave me and made the descent on my knees. The descent is so abrupt that, for the rest, one only has a very feeble notion of what is going on. One sees the light

AT PETROGRAD. 141

of " 36 chandelles," which are certainly not really there!

This slope is succeeded by a flat stretch of ground where the sleigh slackens its pace little by little, losing the acquired speed and so on until it comes to a complete stop. Then one starts all over again.

Once we all—six of us—seated ourselves on a straw mat at the top of the slope. It seemed to whirl round several times on itself during the descent, shedding us to right and left, and finally deposited us lower down pell-mell in the soft white snow.

My cavalier had a costume designed *ad hoc*—*à la Nansen tout-à-fait*. This party ended up by a tea at the Club; and I truly believe that no more warming sport exists.

Every afternoon I spent several hours at the Winter Palace or at the French Embassy, where we worked with energy for the Red Cross, for those unfortunate soldiers who were fighting so far away and also for their families and all they held dear—so far away indeed that one was apt to forget that they were fighting in the same country at all—on the borders of Manchuria. My aunt had presented me at Court, and I was given the privilege—this being a very special favour—of attending, with a number of young girls in society, the daily work parties which were held at the Palace, in the pharmaceutical section, for dispatching parcels to the front.

On my way to the room where we worked

I always encountered Princess Orbeliani—Prince Orbeliani's sister—in her invalid chair; she had entirely lost the use of her feet. She was the favourite maid-of-honour of the Empress, and guarded this favour jealously—as maybe a faithful dog would—but, nevertheless, she was a great nuisance, always watching and scanning the comings and goings of others.

In all the churches on Easter Eve, Midnight Mass is celebrated; and the ceremony is especially beautiful. I was to have attended the service at St Isaac's Cathedral, and had a seat given me amongst those reserved for the Diplomatic Corps, but it was expected that a bomb outrage would be committed, so instead of going there I was persuaded to accompany my aunt to the chapel of the Winter Palace.

The services of the Greek Church are extremely fatiguing, as there are no chairs except for invalids; and the heat on this occasion was so great that the small candles we held melted and bent themselves double.

It is a custom at this Mass to kiss one's neighbour.

In the street, on Easter Sunday, I noticed all the moujiks, country people, and the populace salute one another in the most solemn manner and embracing each other, while uttering the words " Christ is Risen."

There is in Russia a custom which I think quite charming; it consists in the ladies shaking hands with their hostess, while the men and children kiss her hand after luncheon and dinner. A lady does not require much encouragement to kiss the forehead of a gentleman who happens to be on friendly terms with her.

The Catholic churches at Petrograd are always fearfully overcrowded, but soon I gave up going to them, as once at St Catherine's, on the Newsky Prospect, I was literally carried off my feet by the crowd swaying backwards and forwards; and there were very few benches. So in future I preferred going to the Chapel of the Corps des Pages, a college reserved entirely for the young men of the best families destined for a military career, where there was also a Catholic chapel, in which I had been offered a seat, by my Ambassadress, on the benches reserved for the *corps diplomatique*, which was very comfortable

But, before this, I went there once and settled myself in one of the benches belonging to the general public. I knelt devoutly for an instant, but on resuming my seat I realized that I was doing so on some one's knees and not on the hard plank of wood that I expected to find. I turned round to explore the horizon, and what did I find? A stout Polish woman had slipped in behind me while I was at my orisons, and had altogether possessed herself of my seat. I can still see her fat, round face, her heavy, massive figure. One could not dream of using force to dispossess her, and her big victorious eyes gazed at me above their spectacles and the old prayer book, with its pages yellowed by age and its enormous print.

I felt like choking with fury at the sight of all my poor plans for comfort destroyed, and I gave vent to a formidable " Dourak," the only abusive expression in my repertory; a great insult in Russian, and not a very appropriate one, as it means " Imbecile " or even more, and she had not been in the least " imbecile." I ought at any rate to have said " Doura," which is the feminine, but my knowledge of the Russian language was not yet so advanced. It seemed to me that the intruder looked horrified, but sank more than ever into her seat with the air of saying, " J'y suis : j'y reste." It only remained for me to yield her the ground. It was a real defeat.

One of the most interesting ceremonies of Holy Week in this chapel was the procession on Maundy Thursday of the Blessed Sacrament being carried to the tomb, when the four Catholic Ambassadors—France, Italy, Spain and Austria —in full-dress uniform, hold the dais, followed by the Catholic personnel of the various Embassies, also in full dress.

The Austrian Ambassador was the late Count Aerenthal, who has since played such an important political rôle in Austria, and specially during the last few years of his life; it was he who united Bosnia and Herzegovina to the Austrian Crown.

The Italian Ambassador was Count Tornielli, a small man with a good-looking, amiable face;

AT PETROGRAD

the French Ambassador was Monsieur M. Bompard, who played a rôle on this occasion that he would not have dared to play in France!

I often met Prince Hohenlohe, at that time Military Attaché to the German Embassy in Petrograd, and a cousin of the Kaiser's, as well as the chief of His Majesty's spy bureau in Switzerland. It has since been proved that he was a very dangerous one, and had received enormous sums at Paris—where he had also subsequently become Military Attaché—which he distributed to numerous "Bolos"; as for so many people "L'argent n'a pas d'odeur"! He was also present that day, wearing a green plume in the style of a feather brush in his officer's shako.

The works of Leon Tolstoy enchanted me; but for all that I did not like the man who had traced those talented lines. A humbug of the first water, a great Socialist for every one but himself—like most people of his class—Tolstoy had managed to instil his false doctrines into the minds of the students, those thousands of "fish out of water" who are a thorn in the side of Russia, doctrines which caused them to take so energetic a part in the first Revolution also.

May his ashes be agitated in his tomb and suffer at the sight of all the blood spilt, for it is not to be denied that his writings are greatly responsible for the Revolutions which have succeeded each other in Russia; but I fear they rejoice at it!

Possessor of a great fortune, he lived in the greatest luxury, though he posed for poverty and simple tastes, having himself photographed writing his works in a poor cottage for propaganda on post cards, or working himself behind a plough in a field.

Even his death was a final pose. To leave his home to go and die in a railway station, so that he should be talked about to the last! flying from his family and his devoted wife who had helped him so much in his work, and had copied, it is said, eight times the whole of *War and Peace* ; which act certainly denotes the greatest devotion!

CHAPTER XIII

AT that time motors were very rarely seen in Russia, the reason for this being, I suppose, that there were so few good roads; and when one did appear in the streets it immediately became an object of the utmost curiosity.

Another striking feature in Petrograd was that there was not a closed cab to be seen, nothing but little open vehicles, which struck me as being an almost barbarous custom considering the extreme cold of the place. I asked my aunt the reason of this; she told me that the authorities had once tried the experiment of "Voitures fermées—mais il s'y passait tant d'horreurs que l'on avait dû y renoncer."

The tziganes had an enormous success at Petrograd. I went to hear them play one night; their music was quite diabolical and so was the flashing of their eyes. They were the terrors of the mothers, and were responsible for many scandals—and even suicides. They played and sang with so much go and rhythm —it was quite bewildering; the hall was, needless to say, packed to overflowing.

At the time of my arrival in Russia the Dreyfus affair had been and still was the topic of general conversation, people's opinions over there being very diverse; the Protestant element—in England, too, I know—made him a hero and treated him as a martyr, whereas the Orthodox Church considered him a traitor and a renegade, which latter opinion as a loyal Frenchwoman I naturally shared, the opposite sides taking so much to heart their deductions that it was best to avoid touching on the subject altogether.

The Russian woman is, as a rule, very intelligent and well read, a charmer, even if she has no claims to any particular beauty; she is often the man's superior; and in spite of being sometimes a successful butterfly, she is at the same time capable of the greatest attachment and of the most profound devotion.

The Russian man, in spite of his fascination—being very often delightful to meet in society—never inspired me with sufficient confidence for permanence, and I was never able quite to overcome this sentiment.

My Aunt de Baranoff received on Wednesdays, my friends also came to see me that day, and round the welcoming samovar we made our cheerful plans.

Aunt Olga—as I always called her—received in the largest of the drawing-rooms, the ballroom, where there had often been much dancing before her daughter's marriage. In every fine suite of rooms in Russia there is always a ballroom. Round this very large *salon*, lighted during the day by numerous large windows, at night by great chandeliers, were ranged gilded chairs; and great mirrors in panels gave a final note of cheerfulness. The prettiest flowers were always to be found there in profusion, the Court florist coming to change them twice a week, and it was always a real pleasure to see their pretty petals in such bright hues, reminding one of spring and the warm sun, and contrasting so deliciously with the big snowflakes, which in their soft and silent fall, gently drifting against the panes, reminded one of the cold and of the ice from which that frail barrier of glass alone protected one.

Among my aunt's servants there was an old Court man-servant, with a face as cunning as that of an old fox. He was called Grakoff, and moved about without truce or respite in his gold braided gaiters. Unluckily one evening he took it into his head to drink certain pharmaceutical " drops " which my Uncle Peter used to take. Finding them no doubt to his taste, he administered to himself the whole contents of the bottle, so that poor Grakoff was found on the ground more dead than alive, and there was much difficulty in setting him again on his thin old legs—always rather shaky.

On another occasion, I do not exactly know what had passed between him and my dear young cousin, Petia, but the fact remains that Petia came to announce to me with a triumphant smile that he had thrown that old fox of a Grakoff in full dress, with all his gold lace, into his bath, from whence the poor old thing escaped with his head hanging down like a wet poodle. I found this proceeding very Russian—I must admit that it enchanted me—and at the end of the corridor I saw a form dripping from all parts disappearing with all possible speed.

Petia was not entirely without mischief. *Mon Dieu*, he was young and I absolve him. He liked to come home at the latest possible hours, a matter more desired than easy of accomplishment, as my aunt before going to bed used to go and see if the doors were safely bolted. Upon this he asked me to reopen them —later. I refused to do such a thing, and said: " Do what you like ; that is not my business. I promise you I will be discreet, but I will not be your accomplice. Why not ask your old *âme damnée* of a Grakoff ? " But since the unseasonable bath the old *âme damnée* may well have had a pressing desire for vengeance. Petia invited me sometimes to come into his study to smoke one of those delicious scented Russian cigarettes. There were generally some of his friends there, and all set themselves to talk French, with sometimes amusing results.

My aunt continued often to amuse me. One day, having noticed that a certain friend of the family's and I had talked much together, she teased me on the subject. " Oh, aunt," I replied, " that doesn't count, you know quite well he is married." " But, my dear," she said to me, with her kind smile—ce sourire qui savait la vie—" they are the easiest to catch." And she seemed to say, " How naïve you are my poor child!" This answer, in fact, upset all my ideas of life, all the pious doctrines upon which I had been nourished till then.

I thought this power of reasoning quite delightful and typically Russian, disclosing the quantum of moral sense existing out there.

It must be said that divorce is of frequent occurrence in Russia. It is, however, practised by the wealthier classes; as, although the Holy Synod is easy to approach, it knows how to charge!

Couples often so easily disunited, after meeting one another continually in society—for Russian society being very exclusive, is in consequence limited—reconsider their first step and decide to resume their former matrimonial state; therefore, if one has lost touch with one's Russian friends during any length of time, one is obliged to be extremely circumspect on returning to their midst when informing oneself from one member of a family of the rest of his belongings; and it is best to be on the safe side by seeking outside information in the first instance.

Apart from this, however, the other extreme is often to be found, which might be termed of Slavic origin, at least in its outward demonstrations.

I knew a certain Gentleman of the Chamber who lived at the Monastery of La Laure so as to be close to his wife, who had died eight years before and whose remains lay in the cemetery there, going twice every day to pray by the grave—and he was by no means an old man!

Russia being, above all things, a country of contrasts, a country of great extremes, one should not be astonished by any apparent diversity. There, as in the rest of the world, divorce is badly viewed by the serious Protestant community, and, naturally, by the Catholics, but, as the Greek Church authorizes it, one must not judge its votaries too harshly!

The Greek Church is the State religion. If one of the parents is Orthodox, all the children born of that union must belong to that religion, which renders a marriage between an Orthodox and a Catholic practically impossible, since this latter religion also now exacts Catholicism for all the children if one of the parents is Catholic.

It was not so at the time when my grandmother was born, she and her sisters were Catholics like their mother, the brothers Protestant like their father.

In Russia, there is no middle-class as in the West. Society is, in other words, the nobility; and then comes what is known there as the " Merchants," who are absolutely ignored and very much despised by the former, although they are often very rich.

In Russia there were two kinds of caviare, the kind for the *zakouski* and that of the newspapers.

The first is delicious. The *zakouski* is an assortment of *hors-d'œuvres* arranged like a buffet on a table in a corner of the room in which

AT PETROGRAD 153

the lunch or dinner is served. It is partaken of standing up, off a small plate, and amounts, in fact, to a real meal as a preparation to give one an appetite instead of satisfying it.

There is generally fresh caviare and also preserved caviare, and delicious pickled herrings with quantities of other good little dishes, which the men wash down with vodka.

I was extremely fond of this caviare, but did not feel the same affection for that of the newspapers, especially during the Revolution. One of them reached us showing nothing after its title but five lines, and the five last ones! This variety of caviare is a thick black substance; if one tries to scratch it off, it spreads more and more and seems to become more and more opaque.

The liberty of the Press certainly did not exist then.

The Jesuits were not tolerated in Russia, their influence, intelligence, *savoir-faire* and cunning were feared. The Dominicans were looked upon kindly, as well as a few other Orders, and I consider that the exception was really flattering to their Order.

As for the Jews, they were looked at askance. There were no Jews admitted into the army, only a percentage of them were educated in the public schools, and that percentage was very small.

In Russia Jews are not known in society at all; besides, out there, they had not "de-palestined" themselves as with us. Poland was full of them ; at Vilna, for instance, two-thirds of the population were Jewish !

As in England, even more than in England, tea is the drink of the Palace as well as of the *izba*. In this cold country one often needs a hot drink, and the samovar, that really national object with its gentle, warm murmur of boiling water, is the first friend to greet you in a Russian house.

Russian tea is very good ; the green tea is excellent, very scented and very strong. It comes from China on the backs of camels ; therefore, the salt air has not robbed it of any of its first delicacy and strength. A slice of lemon generally replaces the milk and cream customary with us.

Women drink it in a cup, men from a glass in a gold or silver mount with a handle.

CHAPTER XIV

THE French Embassy welcomed me in the most charming way, and I retain the best remembrances of the moments spent in its *salons*. The Russians considered the Bompards bourgeois after the Montebellos, who had lived there *en grands seigneurs*, spending their large fortune, and dipping into it also a little. The Russians would have liked France to send them a marquis, a duke, a prince—considering that more flattering—but at least a "handle." And, as the people who made this remark to me were considered to have advanced ideas, I answered: "But that is democracy; what else do you make of it?" Upon which there was silence.

One evening Madame Bompard told us as a great secret that we must all say how we liked the quality of the tea served that evening, for it had been sent her by the Chinese Minister, who would be there. We therefore all exclaimed on the merits of the liquid—very pale, very scentless, very insipid—which was served to us; the most perfect mixture possible, as it appears, and into which is introduced a great quantity of rose leaves. And the little yellow man was all smiles, swinging more than ever his long pigtail, the antics of which testified to his gratitude.

All the winter that same pigtail, a sort of bell-rope, inspired me with a wild desire to pull it; a desire that I repressed, as one of the secretaries, to whom I had confided my temptation, exclaimed breathlessly: " On no account do that, it would be a *casus belli* ! "

This same little Minister always arrived dressed in the most beautifully embroidered robes imaginable. I have never considered the yellow race outwardly beautiful, but I grant one point of beauty to the Chinese soul, since this same little man told me that the Chinese always wore embroidered on their garments a flower of the season. A pretty idea, and I congratulate them on having retained the custom; it seems to belong to another age.

Among the Russians who attended assiduously at the Mondays of our Ambassadress was Princess X . . . She would never have discovered gunpowder, and her husband even less; but he at least was only to be seen when he dined there, and then he took his departure very early, to go no doubt to more amusing resorts. She, dark, tall and stout in proportion, immensely amused the men by her heavy stupidity, which caused her to say the silliest things. One evening, speaking in a mincing voice, and assuming the *air ingenu* which she particularly affected, she asked them in a foolish way what it meant to say to some one: " Vous êtes une tourte." The little circle began to laugh and wink at each other. She particularly addressed herself at the moment to a certain tall, young secretary of the Embassy, M. de C . . ., who confessed, laughing a trifle nervously, though really delighted, the unflattering suggestion concealed in this word—stupid—for no one doubted that she herself had been thus described; and she was rather sensitive, the dear Princess. He sauntered along gracefully to tell me what had passed, and we chuckled mischievously about it.

This evening, like all others, came at length to an end. Towards midnight every one dispersed like a long and elegant chaplet on the wide red-carpeted steps of the Embassy grand staircase.

At the foot of the last flight C . . ., all muffled up in his thick fur coat, his face half concealed behind his high turned-up collar, his eyes almost buried under his fur cap, found himself face to face with our Princess, still displaying her shoulders, which were always exposed to the fullest advantage.

"What are you carrying, C . . . ? What a bundle!" she said in her loud drawling voice, displaying her pretty teeth and at the same time pointing to a voluminous parcel which the bearer was trying in vain to hide from the general gaze; and, so saying, she wriggled her back caressingly.

"C'est la tourte, c'est la tourte," he said with a feeble smile, and casting a significant glance at us as he disappeared.

In her subsequent conversations she never again referred to "tourtes."

That evening, in the privacy of her sanctum, she must have reflected that there were really too many " tourtes " in this world.

I had a feeling of well-being when from the great *salons* of the French Embassy, and from beneath their gilded panelling, I threw a glance from the great bay windows with double panes on the Quai Français and on that wide and beautiful Neva, so calm, so silent under its double mantle of snow and ice.

The soft warm temperature and the pretty rosy light, the cold whiteness down below formed the most delicious contrast.

Having read Jules Verne's descriptions of floating icebergs in the Arctic regions, for some reason or other one imagines that all very frozen water in very cold countries must convey icebergs, but I was cruelly disappointed at not having my expectations realized to the full on that point at the time of the *débâcle* in Russia and by seeing only huge agglomerations of ice being carried along, all as flat as vulgar pancakes. It seemed an interminable flow as it passed, as not only the Neva freed itself thus of its winter coat, but also the great lake Ladoga; and, watching, one could not help associating all this apparently aimless rush of the ice towards the great salt sea with the passage of life, with all its hurry and scurry—here to-day, gone to-morrow!

At Petrograd the water is—or rather was—undrinkable, and my aunts recommended me never to touch a drop; consequently one is obliged to buy the drinking water at the chemists, who get it at a certain special place.

A most virulent form of typhoid fever is rampant there, especially during the spring at the time of the melting of the ice, when all this frozen mass of winter snow has to be broken up by axes in many places, and on the removal of which many microbes are set in motion. Russia then becomes a veritable sea of mud, which state, however, is almost immediately succeeded by the sudden bursting forth of spring with all that season's richness and loveliness. I felt I actually saw the grass growing, so forcibly does Nature revenge herself. Very few diplomats really liked Petrograd, the cold climate, the expensive life, the absence of light in winter, the light nights in summer, were so many subjects of complaint. It is no doubt *plus chic* to show oneself dissatisfied ; but I who found all delightful, thought this attitude of mind very tiresome.

Among the discontented ones was one of my friends, Marquis de M . . ., Secretary at the Embassy. His father had been in the army under the command of my grandfather. He had brought from France an old family dagger which had formerly been the weapon of a not less valiant ancestor, a Crusader, who had reddened it with the blood of infidels, and his dream was to hunt bears with it, being anxious himself to plunge it into the heart of so stout and dangerous an adversary ; almost a profanation, it seemed to me. I tried, but in vain, to curb this dangerous ardour, being without confidence that my little Marquis, with his small stature and his somewhat flabby air, would emerge victorious from a hand-to-hand struggle with a majestic bear as ferocious as hungry. He stamped with rage and anxiety when explaining that he might, perhaps, not have the luck to find one even if he went to the enchanted spots from which others returned crowned with laurels.

I informed him then that there was a very flourishing industry where a victim was supplied you at the indicated time and place, out there in *le pays des ours*, and he could very easily acquire a skin for a rug; but my Marquis listened with horror to the suggestion of this subterfuge, asking only for the simple glory which he could honourably accept. How many there are less honest who supply themselves with the white skins so easy to achieve.

Nevertheless he dreamt delightful dreams, of hunting Bruin throughout the winter, which were never realized, for very soon he packed up his ancestral dagger and returned to his beautiful country. I saw him again a last time on the eve of his departure, dapper and spruce. "My servants have started, my horses also," he said, laughing, for he possessed neither. "To-morrow it is my turn."

I often teased him about his political opinions, and it was a real joy to see him pose as a republican fanatic.

At one of Madame Bompard's Wednesdays

AT PETROGRAD

some of the ladies took it into their heads to ask the Marquis his Christian name, and each of us played at guessing it. The one who teased him the most was a young and pretty Rumanian —Madame Z . . . Impossible to obtain an answer; very strange, it must have been that name! The most extravagant names of saints flew about. "I know, I know," suddenly cried the young Rumanian lady in her fresh, gay voice. "His name is Joseph." And of course we all yelled out in unison, calling him Joseph. The more he protested, the more we insisted. It seemed to pain him singularly, when suddenly a defender arose. "Joseph, and why?" protested the Dutch Minister from behind his eyeglass. "He has nothing in common with him." None of the ladies dared to continue the subject.

Lord Hardinge, afterwards Viceroy of India, was then British Ambassador at Petrograd. I very much admired Lady Hardinge, who is now no more. His counsellor was Sir Cecil Spring Rice, now our Ambassador at Washington.[1]

The Dutch Minister was a shrewd, distinguished man; he always teased me very much. He had a biting wit and did not lack brains. One day when two of the gentlemen were telling in my hearing a story to which I preferred not to listen, he said to me: "You play the *ingénue's* part charmingly, you ought to be in the Comédie française. I shall remember that in thirty years'

[1] Since this was written Sir Cecil Spring Rice has died while on a visit to the Duke of Devonshire at Government House, Ottawa.

time. The conclusion one comes to is that one may tell you a little more," he said to me mischievously. And another time when I was going to skate, and his secretary had instituted himself my professor, he said: "You are on slippery ground, very slippery, Mademoiselle." This with a glance which he launched above his eyeglass, of which he seemed to have no need, as nothing ever escaped him even without its aid.

He was a good raconteur and I enjoyed talking with him. His wife, also, was charming.

An agreeable couple were Count and Countess Ruggieri-Laderchi, the Italian Military Attaché and his wife. They often entertained and were very pleasant. She was a Russian, *née* Staël-Holstein. She told complacently how a fortune teller had predicted that she would be an Ambassadress. May that happen to her if it is still her wish, as then she would be quite in her rôle; but on leaving Russia she settled down in a provincial town in Italy.

The evenings at General Gelinsky's were also charming; he was a friend of my aunt's, and one met at his house many officers of the Guards and some diplomats.

During nearly the whole of that winter, the German Ambassadress used to display on her head, and nearly as big as it, planted well in the middle of her coiffure, a yellow flower resembling an immense dandelion, the flower commonly called by us in France *pissenlit*.

I told myself that this conception of the fashions must have originated on the banks of the Spree; but yet this headgear did not seem to clash with the rest of her tasteless get-up, for all bore the stamp of Berlin. The Embassy was not beautiful and not well arranged, a succession of little drawing-rooms, which I thought ugly.

My friend Mademoiselle Thecla de Grelle did the honours for her father at the Belgian Legation, and in a very charming manner too. I had some very good times there. She still sends me news of herself from Copenhagen, where she lives now with her brother, Secretary to the Legation.

At Petrograd the *corps diplomatique* formed one large family who met constantly, which was quite delightful.

A charming couple were the Count and Countess Wrangel, who succeeded the Gyldenstolpes at the Swedish Legation. The Count was the Minister; she was French by birth and very amiable. I have met them since in London, where they are still, and where I have always been touched by their kind welcome.

A great meeting place for our set was on the opposite side of the Neva, at the house of a certain lady of foreign nationality, who was very rich and who used to receive a great deal; but I heard lately that she had left her husband and her home for Germany in company with a young Hun who might easily be her son, as she was by no means a young woman twelve years ago, although a very well preserved one and always beautifully dressed. She could have easily been a grandmother even in those days. As in the fable, the deserted husband mounts to the tower to see if there is a cloud of dust on the road; but in vain! If there is any dust, the wind of the Neva is the only cause of it.

The Bulgarian Minister was then Monsieur Stancioff; his wife, French by birth, had been Maid of Honour of the Princess Clémentine, mother of King Ferdinand of Bulgaria, and a daughter of Louis-Philippe, King of the French, who had been married to the Prince of Saxe-Coburg-Gotha as far back as 1843. Ferdinand of Bulgaria, thus being partly French and partly German, had always been considered to have adopted his mother's nationality in preference to his father's, but owing to his second marriage with a German Princess—Eleonora de Reuss—and the promise of great things from the Kaiser, the head of this mushroom Tzar was completely turned in the wrong direction.

Madame Stancioff was a very intelligent woman and certainly without any *préjugés*. One had heard that the Prince had taken a great fancy to her, and after her marriage with a cavalry officer he put him into the Diplomatic service, and so settled him in life. After Petrograd they came to Paris, where the Legation was maintained on a great scale by Ferdinand, who evidently remained faithful to his friends. About the beginning of the war they were appointed to Rome, and I saw in the papers that, being suspected of Francophile tendencies, the Kaiser had asked the renegade Ferdinand not to let them occupy that post any longer. At their house I also received a charming welcome.

CHAPTER XV

RUSSIANS are very superstitious: for instance, they would never tell you that you are looking well, without tapping wood several times with the forefinger for fear that what they said should bring you bad luck. My Uncle de Baranoff, an intelligent and staid man, was a victim to this weakness, and I have sometimes seen him rise from his armchair and cross a large room to go and tap on a piece of wood which he considered suitable when having made a statement of this sort.

In business matters Russians are so slow as to be very trying. I knew many important industrial people, constructors of ships and guns, who were in despair; belonging as they did to an allied but foreign Power, they were nearly distracted.

During the winter one is fed almost entirely on frozen food—which does not suit every one—meat, venison, poultry, eggs, etc. Also every country house possesses an icehouse, a regular little house, where provisions are stored for the winter, when Nature slumbers in that heavy lethargy from which the sudden arrival of spring alone can rouse her. *Gelinotte* is very frequently served, and it is eaten with a sort of

AT PETROGRAD

jelly made from wild berries picked in the woods, which blend very well with the strong flavour that the little birds contract from the juniper berries with which they are fed, and of which they are very fond. These little birds make an unpretentious dish out there, but one which is generally appreciated.

The cooking is very good in Russia, at least in the houses which I frequented; it is also very cosmopolitan, much resembling our own, when our own is good—which is not always the case! It is very substantial, for in that cold country one has to eat a good deal. There are nevertheless some very Russian dishes which one finds nowhere else. Among these I mention *blinki*, a sort of pancake made with sour cream, which is eaten especially at Eastertide, and then *pasca*, a cream cake, eaten at the *réveillon*, which succeeds the midnight mass on Easter Eve. Also there is a beetroot soup, called *borche*, quite red since it is made of the juice of the beetroot and to which cream is added; this is always very well served at the Carlton Hotel in London. There is also a cabbage soup with which a piece of beef is placed on your plate.

Caviare is an almost daily dish, either fresh or preserved; there is often a choice of both.

Minced meats—poultry, etc.—are often eaten, arranged in the shape of cutlets, into each of which is inserted a handle made of bone, decorated with a little bit of ornamental paper, as is often done in France also.

There is one thing which you will never eat at a Russian house, and that is a pigeon! In the snow-covered streets and courtyards, everywhere in fact, flocks of big fat pigeons used to swoop down in great numbers. Pigeons in Russia are considered sacred, and the people place much faith in them, venerating but never eating them. Happy Russian pigeon—how your brethren of the West would envy you if they knew of your good luck!

Champagne seems to flow in rivers in Russia, and all the wine there is very good; French wines are drunk and others coming from the Crimea and the Caucasus, which produces very good vintages.

Cucumbers are also very much eaten, during their season, a specially small kind of cucumber. Every one has his own, and they are passed round the table whole in a great salad bowl, in which there is a little salt water; one cuts it as if it were a pear.

It is usual to find in one's place for lunch and dinner two sorts of bread, one white and one black. I liked the black bread, which was very thick and substantial, for one has a good appetite in Russia.

If life is of the most comfortable and of the most luxurious among rich people, the Russian moujik lives the most primitive existence in his *izba*. In winter, to keep himself warm, he sleeps on the tile-covered stove. The Russian peasant woman has a child every year, but terrible epidemics decimate these numerous families ; scarlatina and diphtheria make awful ravages. In the villages there is a public bath where the moujik goes, but as on coming out he dresses again in his dirty sheepskin, his object seems but half attained. This bath has not the luxury of the sulphur baths at Tiflis ; all of white marble, not only the piscina, but the walls and the floor of the room also. I went one day to see the public bath for women. For all clothing they had only their hair spread out, and reminded me of the story of Genevieve of Brabant.

I remember one young woman whose long black hair fell below her knees. In one hand she held a child of about three, and all the bathers gave me the impression of real Naïades, with their bodies half out of the water, and one wondered whether the rest of them was not fish-like. The masseurs, it appears, are excellent.

I was much struck in Russia by the number of people in the streets who were pitted with smallpox marks to an extent that is quite appalling.

The peasant is well versed in the properties of herbs, the virtue of which he knows, and which he uses with success.

It appears that a certain peasant has discovered an infallible cure for hydrophobia, which is kept as a family secret and which is as regards results quite equal, it is said, to that of Pasteur. Patients come to him from the uttermost corners of Russia, for a mad dog is not as with us an unknown quantity, but on the contrary is rather common. The cure consists in eating a sort of omelet—the ingredients of which contain a certain purifying herb.

It was very necessary in Russia never to be separated from one's passport, which was certainly one's most precious possession. They ask you for it wherever you may be spending the night, the *dvornik*, or porter, comes to fetch it and shows it to the police, and brings it back to you with one more signature on it, for which you have to pay the infinitesimal sum of a few kopecks, or pennies.

During the day a man-servant, more or less covered with gold braid, does the honours of the house when you enter or leave it. He is known as the *Suisse*. The *dvornik*, a primitive person whose name is derived from *dvor* or door, fills the rôle of concierge, and is on duty all night.

One day we left the Hôtel de France in the most brilliant style. We should have felt enchanted· had it not been for the disorderly gait of the horses which drew us, and the want of stability of our fat coachman who really seemed to oscillate on his wide, his very wide base all inflated and wadded even there, as it is the custom for them to be during the cold winter months.

My friend, Madame de Saint-Pair, was taking me with her to pay some calls. It was one of those disagreeable days of thaw when the roads are nothing but pools of brackish water, and the remains of half-melted snow. After having narrowly escaped getting hung up with other vehicles, or upsetting into the heaps of snow which encumbered the road, we arrived at our destination. My friend was going to visit a friend who was ill, and I decided to remain in the carriage, thinking the coachman would keep still—but not at all.

In vain I called to him out of the window—sacrificing thereby my hat—" Stop, stop!" The footman who had got down gave him the same order, but in vain. He had taken it into his head to drive as fast as possible, like the humming-top he seemed to have become, round and round the circular grass plot in front of the house. This narrow space, surrounded by rather high iron railings, inspired me with some fear, as we kept knocking up against this barrier, placed there for the protection of the lawn from incautious pedestrians, and this was the cause of my receiving many unpleasant bumps.

Tired at last of this mad race, he pulled up suddenly, and I enjoyed a period of relative calm, mitigated by the fear of seeing him possessed by some fresh whim, when all of a sudden to my terror I perceived all this wadded mass oscillating once more, seeming more inflated than ever—as I have already explained, the wider it is the more chic it is considered. It shook again and then finally quitted the cushioned seat to fall on one side, into a most strange and comical position, almost suspended. Puzzled,

I ended by hazarding once more my big hat through the window, and, *mon Dieu*, what did I see? My fat, wadded coachman suspended, his arms swaying in the air, his head thrown back, his face convulsed, red almost purple; his lips black with the cold and the vodka, murmuring in a beatifically amiable manner words that I could not catch, as his mouth seemed full of a thick glue. In this cold, and in such a condition, what a predicament to be in!

I seemed to see him already dying "*d'un coup*" as the Russians say when they want to say "of a stroke." I leapt out, summoned the *Suisse*, and with the help of the footman we re-established our intoxicated Jehu on his wide base. I had hardly settled myself again in the carriage, when the same scene took place all over again and the base began to oscillate as though agitated by an earthquake or some invisible spring, and this time it fell so low, so much off the seat, that I asked myself by what miracle it adhered thereto.

At last my friend reappeared. In proportion as he became more torpid from the fumes of that terrible vodka, our fat coachman seemed to swell all the more. In Petrograd there was not to be found I am sure a more ample caftan enclosing a larger individual, and how proud he was of his gold lace, which told every one that he was an Embassy coachman. Well— we did not swell with pride at all in spite of his brilliant accoutrements.

Then it was the turn of our poor footman to

distinguish himself. Earth, snow and water desired him at all costs. On returning to the carriage after leaving some cards, we saw him seat himself, not on the little corner of the seat regretfully conceded to him by his obstructive neighbour, but fair and square into space. We nearly fainted. It seemed to us that the wheels, as they went over him, must have crushed some bones of his frail body. Our driver, more unconscious than ever, his quarters bulging, his head between his shoulders, his great arms stretched out, exciting the two black horses with that guttural cry so typical of the Russian coachman, drove on his course unheedingly.

However, the footman caught us up, but, *mon Dieu*, in what a lamentable state he appeared—paler even than we were and literally covered from head to foot in mud and filth. So ended that memorable drive; how gladly we should have greeted a ukase from the " Little Father " forbidding alcohol.

In winter a little railway is constructed on the ice of the Neva, in a certain place not far from the fortress of St Peter and St Paul, to connect the two sides. I often used to drive on the frozen waters of the river, covered with dazzling snow, in my aunt's carriages. I enjoyed it immensely, and I liked sometimes going to see the ice being sawn into huge blocks, great cartloads of it being taken away.

As the snow freezes as it falls, there is never any necessity to encumber oneself with an umbrella.

One of my diplomatic friends never adhered to this rule and consequently one day he was pursued in the street by urchins yelling out "*Sale Anglais.*" It is here necessary to explain that during the Russo-Japanese war the English did not altogether lie on a bed of roses over there.

He felt doubly innocent of these accusations and could not lay claim to belonging in any way to Albion. He consequently disappeared into the first friendly door he passed, and the umbrella never went out again.

The great secret of being able to support the climate of Petrograd is to wear the same greatcoat every day throughout the winter, whatever the temperature may be, until after what is known there as the *débâcle* of the Neva.

To leave off one's winter clothes before this moment is pure madness. Your winter coat must necessarily be very warm, lined with fur and very thick, with a very high fur collar, which when raised—and it must always be raised—must entirely cover the ears; a fur toque is the most practical head-dress, with one's hair done low on the forehead, as the cold is so intense that it seems to wish to penetrate like a chisel just where the nose begins, between the eyes.

A pair of snow-boots, or a pair of *velinki*—dainty, little fur-lined boots—is indispensable unless one wishes to contract congestion of the lungs—a thing very easily accomplished in that country. When skating, these particular shoes must be warmly lined.

Russians never take much exercise, and they nearly all wear what is known there as the *chouba*, a kind of pelisse lined very thickly and often with the most valuable furs; but I did not adopt this mode, for the good reason that I could not bear the idea of being always smothered up, and I hated its feather-bed appearance.

In winter, every window is hermetically sealed with the exception of one small casement, which is opened for a few minutes only each day, just sufficient to allow a little fresh air to penetrate—so intense is the cold.

It is usual even to fill with sand the space between the double windows—on account of the cold there are always double-windows—up to the height of the bottom of the first pane of glass.

One takes off and puts on one's heavy furs in a specially arranged place just inside the front door of the houses, as it would not be possible to bear the weight of them in the warm atmosphere indoors and it would be sudden death to venture outside without them. Consequently, with these arrangements for one's comfort and with reasonable precautions, there is no country in the world where one need suffer less from the cold than in Russia; not that dreadful penetrating damp cold one continually experiences in French and English houses only fit for snipes and snipers to exist in.

Many martyrs to rheumatism in our countries would not be troubled by that painful complaint in Russia, a fact which must be entirely due to the dry atmosphere of the houses.

Contrary to the general opinion which one hears so often expressed, that the atmosphere of Russian houses during the winter is oppressive, I must say I only once experienced this uncomfortable sensation, and then only on a staircase. I own I was there again spoilt, as my aunts lived in the luxury of spacious and lofty apartments, and all the people I knew did likewise. The doors connecting the different rooms were always left open as much as possible, thus equalizing the warmth of each, which was delicious. Every room had its own large tiled stove; the stoves are closed so that the fire cannot be seen, and they are of the same height as the room, seeming to form part of the wall, which has not an ugly effect, as it is concealed as much as possible. Birch wood was burnt and only required stoking once a day.

To the amazement of my aunts I bore the climate without the least hitch, the secret of which was, I think, the delight I felt at being there—realizing a dream which I had always had, which I had nursed in silence, and cherished as a vision, and which I enjoyed, even more than I had dreamt, as a reality. It seemed as though I had always lived this life that I loved, surrounded by the warm friendly affection which had welcomed me, and as in the song, it was mine to say :—

> " Et le grand soleil qui me brûle
> Est dans mon cœur."

CHAPTER XVI

ON her return to Petrograd for the winter, my Aunt Cherwachidze took up again her charitable rôle of confidante to her protégés, who overwhelmed her with visits, disputed for her favours or her kind looks, paid court to her, were jealous of each other, even hated each other. One of them, Baroness K . . ., a very pronounced type of the real Tartar, with waved black hair, great round black eyes, and lips outrageously reddened, came to see her very often. Her showy toilettes, red and yellow, a relic of barbarous times, made one's eyes ache. A big hat, a real lampshade, generally scarlet, completed a toilette of the most doubtful taste.

Her gait was slow, her feet were much turned out; and as she walked, balancing herself on her heels, slowly and deliberately, the chest out and the head thrown back, she looked rather alarming. Her cousins, real, savage Tartars living in their own country, were always threatening to kill her, in order to possess themselves of her fortune which they believed to be immense. Divorced and redivorced, it really was beyond one's comprehension.

She was the terror of my Aunt de Nicolay —to whose charge especially I had been entrusted—this on my account only, but without any reason for being so as far as I was concerned, for I was frightened of her and always kept at a distance.

Her case seemed to me a bad one, almost desperate!

The next in assiduity was small and plump; she used to arrive dressed as often as not in a tight black voile dress, in the old-fashioned style. Her sleeves of transparent gauze eternally displayed the white skin of her plump little arms, of which she was very proud.

She used to sink into a vast arm-chair, take breath, confer in low tones with my aunt, and then they would both disappear into the comfortable study, the usual scene of confidences. Her confession made, she would reappear, more smiling and plump than ever, and seizing the parchments from which she was never parted began to declaim verses, certainly doomed to perish with her. In vain had she tried to flood the editorial pastures, for the editors proved to be an impenetrable barrier to her literary attempts.

One day she arrived for lunch much too early —my aunt, the little feather of her hat blowing in the wind, not having yet returned—with the added attraction of her son, a young puppy with a fascinating and conquering air. His hair was fair, his face was pink with fairly good features but—I could hardly repress a smile when, looking down, I saw his little form clothed in a frock coat, tightly moulding his figure.

And what a figure, so Lilliputian. Choked by his high collar, he clasped a shiny tall hat in his hands; a pair of gloves of delicate tint and patent-leather shoes completed the accoutrement of this ridiculous little fop.

The lady was dressed that day in canary yellow up to the waist, a bodice very transparent on all sides, the marble of her little arms delicious under the tissue, and her neck! and her throat! and—luckily my aunt was short-sighted!

It fell to my lot to entertain the little dandy, her son, during the whole of lunch. He embarked on every subject with the same self-possession, and when I asked him how he spent his time, and he had answered me over his high collar in a voice necessarily rather choky, " I occupy myself with sport," I felt myself suffocating with laughter. He had lately been doing a little motoring and was consumed with pride, the little puppet!

She, poor woman, had in the Caucasus a husband who had deserted her for another fair temptress, and wished to divorce her—hence these whisperings, this mystery, these tears when she spoke of him. Was there no virtue then in these round and shapely arms?

I do not at all know how my aunt managed it, but the fact remains that when I left Petrograd, the ex-unfaithful one, too, was always there, and husband and wife seemed like two turtle doves. And more than ever the fine, white gauzes fluttered round the white arms and the short neck, and all her plump little being seemed to revel at the restoration of her conjugal rights.

Prince Lucien Murat spent part of the winter at Petrograd. He sometimes took us to see the wrestlers. He had a box there and this entertainment was also a very smart rendezvous. Many officers were there and smart young women. These wrestlers were real colossal masses of human flesh, and most of them bore animal countenances. They began by parading one behind the other in a long file in the arena, then in pairs they wrestled together, he whose back first touched the ground being the vanquished one, and the others in succession. They were of all nationalities. They did not appear to make any real effort, at any rate their movements were calm and slow, but they must have made some, for by degrees one saw their skins begin to shine with heat.

Their costume was of the simplest, a little pair of bathing drawers.

It was forbidden to walk on the quays with a camera, for fear of its containing a bomb. That did not prevent my doing so all the winter without being troubled. Was I then in the good books of the police?

The Russian custom of not addressing others by their family names, but only joining to their Christian names the name of their father, is at first very perplexing for strangers. Thus, supposing your name to be Olga, if your father's for instance is Peter. you will be spoken of as " Olga Petrovna," and so on, really enough to make one's head ache. In the masculine the termination is altered to " vitch," as for example " Petro Petrovitch."

In Russia all luxuries are very dear, but the first necessaries of life are not more so than elsewhere, and my aunts asserted that flats were cheaper than in Paris, where they become very dear when they are of any size. At Easter it is the custom to give delightful little trinkets in the shape of eggs, decorated with a little coloured stone, often real ones. I brought back many of these. That day the dish consisted of boiled eggs, painted red, blue, etc., and all the household ate them too.

I terminated my winter at my Aunt de Nicolay's, continuing with her my social life and met a good many of her relations who were charming.

Sometimes there came to lunch some austere Protestant missionaries, returned from far-off countries where they might have been eaten, had they been more delectable morsels, but where they had escaped from cannibal jaws. Some of them were good and interesting talkers.

Every Monday evening great commotion in the *salons*; the furniture was removed and replaced by benches, and a minister began to speak to an audience composed of male and female students and young girls. This was the favourite work of my Uncle Paul and my Aunt Marie. I, for my part, took myself off to my Embassy that evening, and in front of the open folding-doors, past which I had to go, a screen was set up, behind which I used to slip out, feeling terribly frivolous. The rustle of my dress caused many heads to be turned, and how guilty I felt thus to distract them from the solemn words—all the more guilty as I did not feel much remorse, and one evening in the shadow of this same screen I seemed to see a happy couple there unconscious of all else.

I was urged to go to the celebrated fair of Nijni-Novgorod. Splendid furs were to be found there and at a very reasonable price, it appeared. Several of my friends went; I should especially have liked to see so unique a sight; so much local colour, so picturesque a diversity of types, costumes and customs would have enchanted me.

In Russia the bureaucracy had a very bad reputation, it was said to be very corrupt, but— was it more so than anything else? That was the only question!

The Russian is a fatalist, a little dose of fatalism is perhaps indispensable in life, but it must not be too great. Perhaps that is why they are the victims of the famous "*Nichevo*"—"It is nothing," "It does not matter"—a word which the Russian constantly employs, and which contains all the *laisser aller* of characters there. This indifference is in part responsible for the development of actual events.

Russian is a beautiful language for singing. I have always liked the Russian accent, so melodious, so musical, and liked it to such a degree that I more or less caught it; and, on my return to France, employed it so much when speaking my native tongue that it was said by some, doubtless jealous of this brilliant venture, that I made a pose of it. A happy thought; what would I not now give thus to catch the accent of my adopted country, but alas, it eludes me; perhaps I have lost the art of posing, or perhaps this also is a pose—a long one!

Naturally the name of General Kouropatkin, Commander-in-Chief of the Armies, was on everybody's tongue. The prolonged resistance of Port Arthur engrossed much of the conversation, as was natural. People began by making a hero of its defender, General Stoessel, and a heroine of his wife. We subscribed at the French Embassy to present him with a sword of honour. In later days he seemed to be looked upon as no better than a common traitor. I met the Stoessels once or twice at Petrograd; they both looked very well fed, and I began to doubt their many privations, but of course it may have been a question of temperament, for with some people stoutness is a sign of illness and not of health and good living.

My first experience of a "little corner of English life" occurred at a dinner party at the Napiers', the English Military Attaché and his wife. For the first time I saw wine-glasses placed at the side and not in front of the plate, and I recall my first emotion, not knowing which were mine, fearing a mistake. I hope

I did not drink from my neighbour's glass, but I can hardly be sure that I did not commit myself.

One day before my departure, my Aunt de Nicolay said to me, "I acknowledge that you have two great qualities: punctuality and discretion."

Mon Dieu, punctuality—yes! I had always been trained to it at school and at home, and I still remember the call to order of my father if we had the misfortune to keep the horses waiting a moment at the front door, those precious animals at whose orders, I maintained, one had always to be.

As for discretion? Perhaps it may be thought that it has been a trifle torn on the brambles along the road of life. Oh, very little, not so much as it might have been—not so much as you think perhaps! If there is a need of pardon? Well, give it or do not give it. Give it at least to the child of twenty with her eyes hardly yet opened on life.

I went again to lovely Michaelovka for a little; and it was with a heart as heavy as lead that I turned my back on this country to which I belong in part, on this country which I had learnt to adore, where the sun is so loath to set or to rise, this country of dreams, beneath its glorious spring verdure, again of dreams beneath its snowy white mantle, to this glorious Neva on which I had so often watched the huge barges silently gliding on the still waters, bearing to Petrograd their great loads of silver-birch wood from distant Finland, manned by bargemen in scarlet shirts which gave such a touch of colour and brightness to the landscape.

I felt almost envious of these poetic barges, and longed to float away on one of them ; but, alas, one must not indulge in too much romance in this prosaic age ! " The West " was calling —so, with a broken heart, I turned my back on dear Holy Russia.

And there a last time on the platform of that Berlin Station, beside that train which was going to take me away no doubt for ever, I embraced for a last time my good and dear Aunt de Nicolay, whom I was not to see again.

My heart swelled with gratitude, but I felt too choked to express my feelings :—

"Partir c'est mourir un peu."

Never have I felt this so much as on that day.

Did my aunt understand the tumult in my heart ? I do not know, I do not think so, and in her pretty voice of which I shall never forget the pure, warm accents so full of real affection she said to me, " Renée, you have not consented to recognize the qualities of — and I fear you will regret it." These were her last words, once more she pressed me to her heart, the next moment I was far away.

And when I felt the woods and fields of the Kaiser unroll themselves through the dark night in the contrary direction in which thirteen months before, my heart full of joy, I had seen them flit by—oh, how different it all was.

No I had not been able to—the want of foresight of twenty summers perhaps, but also its frankness! That tall Russian with the pale face, with the blue eyes, of the Grand Duke type—but what was the good of dreaming, and even in that moment I did not regret. It was not, I expect, what Paradise had in store for me.

Part IV
RASPUTIN: HIS INFLUENCE AND HIS WORK

CHAPTER XVII

FIVE or six years ago some Russian cousins of mine came for a short stay to Paris, and for the first time they pronounced before me the name of "Rasputin," telling me of his disastrous influence at Court and particularly over the Empress. "He has persuaded her"—they told me—"that the Tzarevitch will die if she continues to live with the Emperor as his wife, his object being to assure to the enemies of the Romanoffs that their hope will be accomplished and that no other heir will be born to the Emperor, which is their great fear." Besides, at that period the Empress was ill and nervous, and at times could not walk, having to be wheeled about in an invalid's chair; to-day, I am told, she has returned to that chair, in Siberia, whither her unqualifiable conduct has led her.

The Emperor certainly had an heir, and for once rumour was right as to what had indeed happened to the poor child, and he had been made to forfeit the hope of posterity to the line of which he might well be the last member. "Therefore he will not reign," said my cousins. The Emperor had even chosen his successor, a son of one of the Grand Dukes.[1]

[1] The Tzar's brother had at this time been excluded from the succession on account of having contracted a morganatic marriage.

Grand Duke Alexis in addition has very feeble health, and the doctors had doubts whether he would live beyond the age of sixteen, which he has not yet reached. They said that also he was attacked by that infirmity which consists in having a skin too few, and consequently a liability to severe hæmorrhages.

My cousin told me that one day on getting into his bath, the Tzarevitch slipped a little and immediately a great " pocket " of blood formed itself; the same thing occurred one day in stepping out of a boat in which he had been for a sail. In fact the poor boy suffered from a strange and disconcerting illness, which is partly explained to-day, as will be seen later on.

Then I asked who Rasputin was. I was told that he called himself a pope, but in reality he was only a coarse and ignorant adventurer from Siberia; and they spoke with disgust of this intruder and the position he had contrived to acquire.

Rasputin, a name for ever detestable and detested by all who have a grain of feeling of straightforwardness and honesty, is perhaps the most diabolical figure of our century. Some hundreds of years ago he would have been looked upon as a sorcerer.

A native of Pokrovskoe, a little village situated in the province of Tobolsk in Siberia; a mixture of charlatan and satyr; neither monk nor priest, but simply an illiterate peasant; a poor village driver; father of three children left behind in their *izba*, but who later on came to school in Petrograd.

To the most depraved morals he joined a great love of vodka.

After having tried theft several times, and been sentenced to two or three terms of imprisonment, the luminous idea dawned on him one fine day to pose as a saint, thinking the occupation would be more lucrative. He therefore embarked on the life of one of those wandering monks living on alms and of whom I have already spoken.

From the depths of those strange steel-grey eyes came a light endowed with an enormous magnetism, amounting to hypnotism, it seems, and he practised this power on nearly all the women whom he met irrespective of age, surroundings, disposition, bent of mind—whether light or austere.

Naturally he employed this power to surround himself principally with women in the best society, and also with those endowed with large fortunes, this being at the same time more flattering and more practical.

The new religion, if one may so describe the lax and too easy doctrine that he preached, was, I am told, a mixture of those " religions " that flourished in the Middle Ages, and appealed to that *milieu* enormously. He went so far as to preach that a laxity of morals should be regarded as the sin most easily pardoned by the Almighty . . . and women of the best-known families and those placed in the highest position were present incognita at these " religious " services.

During each of his so-called "pilgrimages" he continually made new disciples; sister-disciples thronged his progress.

It was at one of these meetings at Petrograd that Madame Vyruboff, of unlucky memory, who is to-day imprisoned in the fortress of St Peter and St Paul but who was then the favourite lady-in-waiting to the Empress—in fact the most intimate confidante of both the Tzar and the Tzarina—met him for the first time. This intriguer, like so many others, fell so much under his influence that she became one of his most zealous and devoted followers —later she became his mistress—and formed the project to present him at Court.

All the same, this was not brought about without a certain amount of trouble and delay, for the scoundrel, who at the bottom of his heart trembled with joy at the mere notion of this presentation, required pressing, and even gave the impression of rejecting the idea, refusing to accede to it on the pretext that he made no difference between the lowest of the moujiks and the great ones of the earth.

He had then arrived at accomplishing "miracles"; his reputation of "miracle worker" had already been established, and was spreading each day, gaining ground like a spot of oil. Thanks to his ingenuity and to that of an accomplice, he had continued to create the appearance of effecting some.

Madame Vyruboff, knowing how vital to the Empress was the question of the health of the

Tzarevitch—to whom she wished at all costs to assure the throne of the Romanoffs, in spite of the early death which the doctors had foretold for him—had the " brilliant " idea of first presenting Rasputin, the intriguer, believing that by so doing she would make herself useful and important, conjecturing also that he might perhaps do something to ameliorate the health of that frail being.

The rascal pretended to hesitate, but consented at last, on receiving a message from the Empress asking him to come and visit the little patient. He was received with all the eagerness, all the ardour that can be felt by a maternal heart which has borne a long agony of pain and anxiety, and when she saw him stretch his hands over the frail little body of her child in the act of blessing, and thus perhaps produced a healing influence, she, too, while weeping grateful tears felt herself fall under the influence of the strange fascination which he exercised, above all, when turning to her, with that particular manner which made a victim of nearly every woman he met, he promised her a complete cure.

And the Tzarevitch, as though to lend more weight to his words, seemed to show an improvement after the visits. The Empress, full of hope, only saw in this charlatan a saint, a messenger from Heaven sent to cure her child !

From that time Rasputin took root in the palace and began to " instruct " the ladies of the Court ; the practical side was not forgotten by him, and if he had made dupes he had also reaped a great harvest of money. He pretended to collect for the monastery built by him in his native village, where the monks lived an austere and most ascetic life of prayer among the most luxurious surroundings, the fruit of the offerings collected by him.

From time to time he would threaten his "sister disciples" to leave the capital and return to the monastery, at hearing which they became desolate, and one and all implored him to remain.

The Empress, more than anyone, was petrified at the thought of what might happen, and all the more that, each time that Rasputin went away, a change for the worse was noticed in the health of the precious child.

This may be explained thus: Rasputin was well versed in the composition and effects of certain drugs known in the East, which he obtained from a great friend of his, an Oriental quack doctor, who gave to his patients infusions of herbs brought from Tibet, and he took care to have one of them administered to the Imperial child by Madame Vryuboff when he was absent. This, while making him ill, assured Rasputin's recall, and as may be imagined he was not anxious to cut short his brilliant career. Sometimes it happened that the drug brought the child apparently too near the gates of death. Hence the short despairing and heart-rending notes, of which so much has been said, addressed by a poor distracted mother to the "Saint"!

RASPUTIN: INFLUENCE AND WORK

He made himself even more needed, and did not even reply to the Imperial missives. Then, tiring of the charms of his so-called beautiful and austere monastery, which had never existed, and was in reality but a poor house where his family lived, and, in addition, twelve of his admiring and fanatic "sisters" and where he had, as one may imagine, a lively time, he would reappear, and be greeted as a saviour.

The Tzar did not like Rasputin, but he tolerated him. His Majesty generally possessed a clear judgment, but never had quite the courage of his opinions; and unluckily his courage stopped short of sending the rascal away.

Among the friends of Rasputin must be mentioned Protopopoff, Minister of the Interior, and Boris Sturmer, who thanks to the former's intrigues had been appointed Prime Minister of Russia. Both were known to be pro-German.

The "monk's" empire at the Court became so great that through the intermediary of the Empress those who had been remiss to him in any particular lost important posts, and he also caused his unworthy "protégés" to be given the highest appointments. This grew to such an extent that he really came to out-Emperor the Emperor himself, and he knew it—that shameless rascal who endeavoured to make himself look like the picture of Christ.

He had also powerful enemies, among whom was Stolypin, an honest man, and then one of the most powerful men in the Empire. When in 1906 the New Russian Imperial Duma assembled for its first session, the question of the redistribution of land became at once the chief topic of the debates. The second Duma took it up also, and after the dismissal of the second Duma the Government considered the same question again. Monsieur Stolypin, who was Prime Minister at the time, introduced his very much discussed Land Reform Bill, which provided to a great extent for the distribution of State and Crown land to the peasantry; but this land reserve was big and would not have been exhausted for a long time. The chief object of Monsieur Stolypin's land reform was to break up the communal ownership. There was no appropriation of private owner's land and no private owner was forced to sell his property. As a result, 2,000,000 new farms sprang up in different parts of Russia. Later on, he also paid for his honesty, like so many others, by perishing from a bomb explosion at Kief.

But the enemy Rasputin feared most of all others was Grand Duke Nicholas, who had learnt a great deal about the so-called "Saint" and esteemed him accordingly; Rasputin knew this and was consequently not free from anxiety. I have been assured that at a ball given at the Palace since the War, the Grand Duke Nicholas, assisted by young Grand Duke Dmitri Paulovitch, seized the mock monk, who naturally was there, the pupils of his eyes more charged with magnetism than ever, and tearing off the pious emblems with which he was covered—

one more fascination—administered the most severe chastisement after having thrown him outside.

Soon after the commencement of hostilities Grand Duke Nicholas was appointed by the Tzar Commander-in-Chief of the Russian Armies on the German frontier. Later on, he was appointed Viceroy of the Caucasus and the Tzar took the full command of the Western front upon himself. It was an established fact that the Grand Duke's transference—which became a burning question—was brought about entirely by the influence of the pro-German group by which the Emperor was surrounded, these intriguers finding the presence of the Grand Duke a great obstacle to the realization of their dark plans.

A great sportsman, the Grand Duke had the best pack of hounds in the Empire; his borzois were unrivalled in beauty, strength and speed, and he possessed wonderful shooting preserves in the Caucasus and elsewhere.

Following on the Tzar's abdication, it was decided by the existing Government to reinstate the Grand Duke Nicholas as Commander-in-Chief of the army, in which post he had so greatly distinguished himself at the beginning of the war; and he was actually on the point of leaving for head-quarters when the Committee of the Workers' Delegates and the Committee of the Soldiers' Deputies, egged on by the Socialists, protested against the measure. The Labour Party were alarmed that the great popularity of the Grand Duke with the army might be the cause of their proclaiming him Tzar of Russia; therefore they insisted on the revocation of his appointment, and Kerensky upheld them, threatening to resign from the Cabinet should the Grand Duke assume the Chief Command.

From the appearance of Rasputin, Germany was on the watch, realizing what an easy prey Russia might become, and soon the pockets of the " Saint " were bulging over with German gold. Surrounded by pro-German friends, they began to plot for Germany to such an extent, and so successfully, that Rasputin was sent for to Berlin by the Kaiser, who it may be imagined did not waste his time. Rasputin, installed in a fine house near the Moika, saw his religion develop every day; then it was that Grand Duchess Olga, the eldest daughter of the Emperor, became one of his most fervent " sister disciples," and on his return from his clandestine journey to Germany, in 1916, he began cleverly to insinuate to his admiring female listeners that a separate peace would be very profitable to the great Russian Empire.

It was in vain that Grand Duke Nicholas and others informed the Empress what Rasputin really was, and told her of his depraved life and his false miracles, it was in vain that they told her that he and his friends would destroy Russia—all these efforts of persuasion were of no avail.

In vain, also, Grand Duke Nicholas implored the Emperor to banish from the Court all those

Germans by whom he was surrounded, telling him bluntly, "If you do not do so, the House of Romanoff is doomed."

As for Rasputin, feeling himself tracked down like a wild beast, he continued to terrorize the Empress on the subject of the Tzarevitch, saying : " If any misfortune happens to me, the Tzarevitch will die too, and that exactly forty days, hour for hour, after me." Many people disappeared and died in a mysterious manner, many dramas took place even in the " Saint's " house—and some of these, it was said, were by his own hand—but he always succeeded in suppressing the scandal.

A young woman returned from Petrograd, who had the good sense not to become his victim, has told me how she was invited not very long before his tragic end to a tea-party at which the scoundrel was to be present. He entered the room not only with a most self-satisfied air, but one which tried to be also mystical, and began to speak to each of the young women in his hideous jargon, staring with that hypnotic look, which made each one of them his own, at the same time kissing each on the lips, with an incredible and repulsive audacity, as if it were due to him. The witness in question avoided the same fate but with difficulty, upon which the " Saint " took on a puzzled anxious expression, and began to turn round, saying that he felt a current of antipathy in the room and came to a stop in front of her.

From the moment she entered the room

Rasputin did not appear to be at ease, no doubt because of that contrary current.

He seemed to this young woman to be a coarse creature, not even knowing how to express himself; naturally with no manners, and repulsive in his fatuousness; less than well cared for in his appearance, in fact—abject. Only one thing about him was right—of very fine quality—his linen. The Empress, it is said, gave him these very fine shirts; and, when her children were ill, it is said that she insisted that they should wear the " holy tunics " of the " Saint " so that they should not get worse.

It was in 1916 that the power of the mock-monk attained its zenith.

Naturally on the occasion of his visit to England some years ago, the German Emperor and his suite—cunningly chosen with a view to such functions—were there as spies, and not, as so many naïve people believed, as friends.

Prince Henry of Prussia repeated one of his spying tours and many other Germans avowed their love for England publicly—and that with good reason. Those journeys must have been very profitable for them, and I myself have no confidence in those who are alway reiterating the small amount of interest they take in our country, while living in it all the time—what then are they doing in it?

Among the number of those spies one must evidently also count the Queen of Greece, sister of the Kaiser, who at Eastbourne on the eve of the declaration of war, pretended to know nothing about it, notwithstanding which she managed to escape just in time. She must therefore have been informed beforehand, or at any rate at the last moment. Since then she has but too much proved herself a fond sister for it to be possible for us to be credulous; it is true that her affection has cost her her throne, much it is said to her fury. In gratitude the Kaiser, directly on her arrival in Switzerland, opened an account at a Swiss Bank for her to the amount of £50,000.

Naturally, as the secret agent of the Kaiser in Russia, Rasputin was in constant communication with Berlin. They wished to get rid of Brusiloff, then of Korniloff, but failed in the two attempts at assassination, which annoyed Berlin very much. What they desired was the cessation of the great and victorious offensive.

Monsieur Goutchkoff, director of the Committee of War Industries, denounced the " Holy Father " Rasputin to the Duma, but again he managed to escape the consequences, and informed the Emperor that Heaven would certainly take revenge on him and on his heir for what he himself had to endure.

And the poor deceived Emperor did not in the least suspect that Protopopoff was a traitor —that Protopopoff, who had come to England, announcing himself as a friend, and then had gone to France, being received everywhere with a warm welcome—refusing to believe the man to be so double-faced.

Then the "Holy Father," as he was called, told the Emperor that he would do well to mistrust Brusiloff, whom he knew to be a traitor to his country, and insisted on this to such an extent that the brave general was on the point of being arrested a few days later.

He also poisoned the Emperor's mind against Nebrasoff, the Minister of Communications, who was dismissed, being a powerful obstacle to the pro-German clique, and hindering their projects of internal disorganization; for they dreamed not only of bringing about famine in different parts of Russia, but also of sowing there, as well as at the front, the most severe epidemics, the dangerous germs of which were sent with great care from Berlin, and distributed in the food in the more populous districts, so that the result should cause greater ravages. No excuses can be found for the Empress, for I am assured that Rasputin showed her every line of the correspondence sent and received in exchange between Berlin and her many agents. Not only did she acquiesce in their intrigues, but she incited them to more, encouraging them to make a separate peace, and also to sow epidemics and to create famine; and all the while German gold flowed into the hands of this clique.

Nevertheless, Brusiloff had recommenced his offensive, his successes being followed with anguish at Berlin. Sturmer forced Rumania to enter the war, knowing that she was not ready. It was easy to invade her in spite of the valour of her brave troops, and Russia forgot one by one the promises made to her new Allies, and did not come to her help. Then came the great retreat, fruit of the intrigues of traitors. Certain Russian generals had also joined the side of the traitors. Mackensen won easy laurels, and Sturmer, Protopopoff, Rasputin and Co. hoped that the great retreat and the invasion of Rumania would decide Nicholas II. to make that famous "separate peace." These tools of Germany, these creatures of the Kaiser's, hoping for its accomplishment, were delirious with joy.

Sturmer deceived his allies, talking loudly of "no separate peace," while, as is known, he was using all his energies in a contrary direction.

But if the Court and so many of the great ones of the earth knelt before Rasputin, they did not all do so, and the masses had no belief in him. They laughed at him, and this rascal, who knew more than anyone the blackness of his own soul, went about protected by a coat of mail, for he was not without anxiety as to what Fate had in store for him. If his days sometimes gave the illusion of a veneer of piety, his evenings were those of a libertine; and, if the women had gone mad about him, the fathers, husbands and brothers had a mortal grudge against him.

In Kerensky, a lawyer and a member of the Duma, all this vermin scented danger; they wished to be rid of him, aware that he knew rather too much about their secret acts and their profits. An attempt was made to assassinate him in the street, but this fresh scheme of murder failed.

Then followed the accusations, but too well justified, against General Sukhomlinoff. Grand Dukes Nicholas, Dmitri and Serge got to work, and wished to make the allegations public, for matters would have been revealed, strangely deplorable, strangely compromising, for the clique of the " Saint " and his creatures, so much so that it would have meant without doubt the end of their reign, and their anxiety was therefore great. This trial, again by their intrigues, was deferred by the Emperor, and was only opened up again since the fall of the latter ; the General has been condemned to imprisonment for life, on the grave charges made against him when Minister for War.

The respite of the traitors was, however, not of long duration, for Monsieur Miliukoff, supported by the same Grand Dukes, conceived the project of unmasking the "Saint" before the whole Duma. In vain was it tried to prevent him, to arrest him, to kill him ; he was able to escape from the nets spread for him and all attempts failed against this new subject of their apprehension, who, in a packed hall, before most of the Ambassadors, and under the Presidency of Monsieur Radzianko, made that memorable interpellation unveiling what Rasputin and Co. really were, and gaining the applause of the house—November 14, 1916—

and the expression of a unanimous desire, as it seemed, for the continuance of the war.

All Petrograd was stirred. There was a rush for newspapers, but these, being censored, told nothing ; private propaganda were organized to make known the truth, and the speech was distributed in a complete form.

CHAPTER XVIII

MONSIEUR RADZIANKO, as is known, was elected President of the third Duma, and again of the fourth, that is to say, he was President at the moment of the Revolution. He married a Princess Galitzine, and was formerly in the Chevaliers-Gardes, considered the first Russian regiment. Adored by the peasants on his great estates, he was much in touch with the Zemstvo Party, the friend of the peasants. A great friend of Sir George Buchanan, our late Ambassador, his dream for his country was to have a ministry appointed by the Tzar, though outside the Duma, responsible to and dependent upon possessing and retaining its confidence.

The Empress, in the Palace, breathlessly awaited the result, devoured with anxiety as to the issue which none of them had known how to prevent.

The "Saint," seriously alarmed by the revelations of Miliukoff—the only topic of conversation in the capital—thought it prudent to make himself scarce again, and departed on a so-called "pilgrimage."

The Empress was in a terrible state, not only on account of the interpellation, but because since the departure of the scoundrel the condition of her precious child seemed to have become worse every day; hence a desperate summons to return. Madame Vyruboff had evidently received orders to drug the poor boy to such an extent that his condition should be sufficiently serious to madden the poor anxious mother.

The result of the denunciation was the fall of Sturmer; but he received a post at the Palace. He was replaced by Trepoff, an honest man, who at once announced his plan of action: " No separate peace, and war on German influence."

Nicholas II. had not the least idea that Rasputin was the creature of the Kaiser, and though his instinct did not allow him to regard him with any favour, he bore with him, as I have already said, for the sake of the Empress and to avoid family scenes; as he admitted on one occasion: " I would rather put up with this man than have to endure five attacks of hysterics a day."

It is certain that Alexandra Feodorovna was ill, and that her nerves were more than shaken; action should have been taken and on this pretext she should have been sent away. One must admit that there was enough to make her ill. Almost ever since her marriage, in any case since the year before the first Revolution, she lived in constant anguish, asking herself continually what was going to happen to her husband and children; as regards that one cannot blame her—on the contrary. It is said that the Empress has sent her magnificent jewels to Darmstadt, her native country, to help the Germans continue the war.

Another dangerous spy of the Kaiser's at Petrograd was Grand Duke of Mecklenburg-Strelitz, on the best of terms naturally with Rasputin, and also exercising a great influence at the Palace and over the Empress. He had naturalized himself Russian in 1914; but who is more to be mistrusted than one who has been " naturalized " ?

It was then—at the end of November 1916—that Rasputin was more especially warned that a plot had been made against him. The Grand Duke Nicholas tried again to instil sense into the Emperor, but in vain. And the scoundrel paraded the so-called visions which he had never had, alarming the Empress more and more on the subject of her son, and continuing his work of threatening his approaching death if the famous separate peace were not signed. The Empress had come to believe that if this peace did not immediately become an accomplished fact the Romanoffs were doomed; and this she wished to prevent.

Germany naturally wished much for this peace; but to-day has to use the greatest circumspection before accepting the proposals of Lenin, whose government is recognized neither by the Ambassadors of the Allied powers nor by the Russian Ambassadors in Allied countries.

The dark forces did their best to spread cholera amongst the troops at the front, an epidemic that was luckily stamped out almost at once, to the great disappointment of those who had instigated it. They then tried to poison the Grand Duke Dmitri; but that also failed.

On the 16th of December 1916, Rasputin was invited by Prince Felix Yousoupoff to spend the evening in his father's mansion, under the pretext of meeting a young woman who ardently desired to become a "sister disciple." What I do not understand is, why he should have accepted the invitation, for he had been so often warned against his would-be host. He therefore arrived at the Prince's luxurious house, and was received by him, but after a gay supper was left *tête-à-tête* with one of the Prince's friends on the pretext of inspecting some *objets d'art* which had attracted his notice previously.

The friend in question did the honours of the princely house with affability, and offered Rasputin wine—into which a strong admixture of poison had been introduced!

The mock-monk sipped a few drops in the manner of a connoisseur, which indeed he had become, having accustomed himself to the taste of the famous vintages of the Winter Palace, and then addressing himself to his interlocutor he appeared to be interested in some special work of art on one of the tables in the room, which the latter felt obliged to show him for closer inspection. On returning to Rasputin's side he noticed the monk had become paler as he passed his hand across his face as if desirous of concealing a strong pang of pain.

The Prince's friend positively held his breath, keeping his eyes fixed on his prey as he noticed the glass standing empty beside him; he imagined the inevitable was bound to follow quickly, as the dose was a very strong one.

Upstairs, anxiety grew apace, many hearts were palpitating, every one counting the seconds which seemed eternal. Prince Felix Yousoupoff was there with a few friends who had all sworn to purge Russia, once and for all, of her evil genius.

But, as it happened, at the end of a few minutes the momentary sensation of discomfort seemed to disappear and the rascal became quite himself again to the Prince's friend's amazement, who began to wonder whether after all this extraordinary man opposite him was in reality entirely like other men, and not, as some people affirmed, a demon or a sorcerer, gifted with some wonderful and unknown power of resistance. This man who had the power to heal had also the facility to kill, so it was generally believed. And there, in that room, the silent witness of so many festivities of the past, was about to be enacted the last scene of one of the greatest dramas which had ever taken place in the world's history.

Driven at last almost to despair, the hero of the plot, anxious to conclude his task, drew out his revolver and shot the " Saint " as he gloated over the beautiful antiques; but, although wounded, Rasputin still had sufficient strength to stagger into the hall and was on the point of making his way to the street door as, pale with pain and foaming with rage, he yelled out: " For you have tried to kill me, I will revenge myself." Upon which the hearer renewed his attack, emptying the contents of his revolver into the " Saint's " head—and breathed again freely once more, as this time the " monk " was indeed dead. Then was uttered one general shout of joy from the little group of the Prince's friends assembled not far off, although in concealment during the tragedy. Rasputin had fired several times, but, as he was very drunk, I was told he only killed a dog.

Prince Felix Yousoupoff, on hearing the first shot, had rushed down the stairs and discharged his revolver; but it is said that owing to nervousness his hand shook and missed proper aim, and it was his friend who gave the *coup de grâce*.

It was afterwards discovered that Rasputin, profiting by his companion's momentary absence, had emptied the contents of his glass into a vase on one of the pieces of furniture which stood close by; this, either from distrust or because he had already indulged in too numerous libations.

It has been said that Rasputin was only killed in order to make clear whether it was really he who was guilty of all that had happened, or whether things would go on the same after his death. But it seems to me that his death came too late, and his evil work had been so well started that with or without him matters could no longer move up against the stream—they could only follow the current on which they had been started.

And there, in the great Neva, all black in the dark night, they threw beneath the ice the body, at last reduced to impotence, of him who had been the bane of the great Empire, cold in death as the deep icy water that engulfed it.

During a whole week every one wondered what could have become of Rasputin and why he had disappeared so suddenly and mysteriously; the Court *camarilla*, his friends and the pro-German coterie were at their wits' ends concerning him.

When the body at last was found, the Empress came to prostrate herself before the remains, showing the most violent sorrow, going afterwards each day to pray at his tomb and invoking the most terrible vengeance on his murderers.

These had been traced; and Nicholas II. left her free to inflict on them whatever punishment she chose.

The Grand Duke Dmitri was sent to the Persian front, and Prince Yousoupoff and his son were exiled to their estates, for it was not at that time easy to inflict a heavier sentence on such important people as the Grand Duke and his accomplices.

The Empress could not indeed by punishment slake the thirst of her soul for vengeance, and the unhappy mother was maddened by dread,

RASPUTIN : INFLUENCE AND WORK

only increased with the passing hours, of the realization of the sinister words of the dead man : " If disaster happens to me and I die, the Tzarevitch will die forty days, hour for hour, after me ! "

The hour of the Revolution of March 10, 1917, struck ; the Emperor being at the time at the Front, the moment had been well chosen, or rather arranged. The red rag of revolt was carried in triumph above the heads of a delirious crowd ; ensigns on monuments and everything that could recall an Empire were burned in the great fires lighted in the streets. The Emperor started to return precipitately to the Empress and his children at the Palace of Tsarkoe-Celo, where all the Imperial children were suffering from measles. His first thought was of resistance, and to send his troops against the rebels of Petrograd.

The Grand Duke Nicholas, then Commander-in-Chief in the Caucasus, and General Alexieff, Chief of the General Staff, siding with the Duma, insisted on the abdication of Nicholas II., seeing in that act the only chance of salvation for Russia, and accordingly telegraphed their decision to Miliukoff who had just been appointed to the Ministry of Foreign Affairs.

The nation knew little or nothing of the course that events had taken, and the abdication was only the desire of a few scores of men ; now, many deem it a great mistake.

Generals Russky and Brusiloff also telegraphed to Miliukoff, stating the adhesion of the armies to the new regime, and declaring that all was well.

Grand Duke Michael-Alexandrovitch, brother of Nicholas II., was nominated Regent, but without delay made it known that he would only accept the Regency with the approval of the people. This never came; of course the people did not have a chance of expressing an opinion; Kerensky seized the reins of government and what followed is only too well known.

At first every one was contented with the Revolution; it was hailed as a saviour by those who thought themselves free from the pro-German clique. Matters went well, everything seemed new-born, but when once anarchy broke through its bounds faces began to lengthen, and a feeling of despair arose—which feeling has gone on increasing ever since.

To-day in the depths of her exile, and in her invalid's chair, Alexandra Feodorovna wears mourning for happier days, in the depths of that Siberia to which she never dreamt she herself would be deported one day, that Siberia that she at least has so well deserved by her ignoble treachery, and where she has been sent as a precautionary measure in case of a reactionary movement. And there near the birth-place of her hero now dead, she still mourns more than all else the disappearance of the " Saint." " All this was bound to happen," she says. " It is the just vengeance for the ' Holy Father,' the Romanoffs must end and perish." The Russian people accused the

PLOUGHING IN THE CAUCASUS

THE IMPERIAL PALACE OF TSARSKOË-CELO

Empress of bringing bad luck to everyone; but even at Darmstadt she was considered a bird of ill-omen.

As for Nicholas II. he has become completely imbecile, if rumour is correct, and will never recover his reason; the best thing that could have happened, perhaps, as far as he is concerned.

During his imprisonment at Tsarkoe-Celo, the revolutionary party was obliged often to change the soldiers who guarded him in order to be sure of their fidelity to the new regime, so great was known to be the ascendancy of the " Little Father " over his soldiers.

When he left the Palace for exile, many people knelt and piously crossed themselves as he passed, just as they would had they been shown a holy picture with miraculous powers. That which had been the religion of these humble people, they retained still for their Emperor who was losing his throne through his family affections, obstinacy and weakness.

The outcome of the first Revolution had for result the creation of the Duma, which was intended to be the Saviour and Regenerator of the Empire—it has witnessed its end. Gapon, the idol of the masses, the precursor of Rasputin, appears no more but as a shadow pale, and fugitive.

The outcome of the second Revolution has been the fall of the Romanoffs and the institution of a self-styled Republic, which it was said would bring glory in the field of battle and happy liberty to a great people. I never believed it.

May the damaged walls of the Kremlin express to this great people—whose passions were being let loose at the same time that they were being deceived—the shame felt by them at the sight of the blood spilt around them, blood shed among brothers by a Revolution which has brought them only a civil war and mortal struggles, and will soon have produced more victims than all the Romanoffs together have done with their sentences of exile to Siberia—many but too well deserved, though accounted to them as a crime.

May a Romanoff worthy of the name that he bears rally the real Russia—she who endures and is silent, not being able to do more for the moment—and so make of her again a great power worthy of respect and gaining it, the terror of her ignoble neighbour, Germany—and not her vassal.

That is my most heart-felt wish, and also my most sincere prayer for that great country which is a little mine, and which from the bottom of my heart I love as my second country.

Inquire of an anti-Semite the meaning of the Russian Revolution, and he will expose to you the whole of the Jewish drama which unfolds itself in all its force before you. It is a fact that ever since the Revolution of March all the various Governments which have succeeded each other so rapidly have in every instance been profitable to the Jews only and have done

RASPUTIN : INFLUENCE AND WORK 219

their utmost to upset all the opposing barriers which the *ancien régime* had deemed good for Russia—by setting these up as a rampart against their invading greed. Now that General Allenby has accomplished what Richard Cœur de Lion and the whole of Christendom failed to do—namely, the conquest of Jerusalem from the Turk—it makes one hope that the time has come about for them all to *s'en aller caravaner* back whence they came so many centuries ago.

" Lorsque la grande guerre ou le grand soir révolutionnaire auront passé sur le monde, il ne restera plus dominant toutes ces ruines que la Banque juive."

The above is a quotation from the great Russian author Dostoievsky, which my father, Monsieur Gaudin de Villaine, Sénateur de la Manche, and one of the most valiant leaders of the Right in the French Senate, has made use of on more than one occasion in his interpellations when addressing that body and in an article which was of course boycotted by the Press. It seems to justify itself more forcibly every day.

With the exception of Lenin, who is not a Jew and whose real name is Ullianoff—others say Lehrann and that he is a German—all the members of the Direction of the Soviets are Jews sailing under assumed Russian names. Thus, Trotsky's real name is Braunstein and that of the miserable wretch Zenovieff, who is one of the most active German agents, is really Apfelbaum—and so on !

Lenin comes from a revolutionary stock, his brother having been hung in 1887 for conspiring against the Tzar Alexander III.

I have some Russian cousins living in Italy, where they have been for a great many years, and I hear that according to Lenin's laws they are considered as emigrants, consequently their property in Russia has been confiscated, and should they return they would be imprisoned.

Krylenko, appointed by Lenin as generalissimo of the Russian Army, is a man of very mediocre intelligence; he was up to a few months ago residing near Montreux in Switzerland and was merely a lieutenant of the reserve of the Russian Army. He is not a Jew, but he is known by his friends as Father Abraham, a sobriquet of which he is very proud.

The great Russian people appear to me like a huge ball sent helter-skelter, rolling down a slide from an eminence—the slide is the Revolution.

One Government will continue to replace another until the abyss of anarchy is reached. Germany's plan and interest are therefore to help all the smaller separatist non-Russian people, Finland, etc., to stand on their own feet as free political entities and autonomies.

May this revolutionary night not delay much longer to envelop the country of the German Kaiser, whose greatest pleasure seems to be in shaking and overturning the various thrones of the earth in order to consolidate on their ruins his own—a dangerous game to play, for the revolutionary mirage develops into a very virulent germ once spread amongst a discontented populace.

This Emperor of whom a German diplomat before the war once said jokingly : " If he goes to a christening he wants to be the child ; if to a marriage he wants to be the bridegroom ; and if to a funeral he wants to be the corpse ! "

To-day this Emperor has been nick-named the " Red Kaiser," the War Kaiser, the Kaiser of the Ruins, the Kaiser of the Massacres, and of all the horrors which have been committed.

But, vengeance will come, and justice will make itself felt. Sooner or later, vengeance must come.

That which is not generally known, but what I know authoritatively, is that France might have obtained for herself and her Allies a separate peace with Austria. The brothers of the Empress of Austria were educated in France and are very French at heart, they had gone so far as to open peace negotiations through the intermediary of the Vatican, and all would have gone well had it not been for the regrettable pride of the Italians and the Masonic Lodges !

And· to-day, December 1917, before closing these pages, I look back once more in the direction of the dear great Russia and I salute her ; there, towards the great Steppe beneath its almost perpetual whiteness, where the silence makes itself felt ; towards the luminous and pure atmosphere of the beautiful country of the Don Cossacks, where there seems still to be a ray of hope, perhaps, if only it could assert itself and render back to the moujik his religion venerated in his *izba* during centuries past, not only his sacred pictures, but afar, in a dream of purple and gold his God, his All—a Tzar!

www.ingramcontent.com/pod-product-compliance
Lightning Source LLC
Chambersburg PA
CBHW031425150426
43191CB00006B/403